WOMEN'S HOME DIY

First published in May 2011
Reprinted January 2013
Reprinted in paperback May 2016

British Library Cataloguing in Publication Data
A catalogue record for this book is available from
the British Library.

ISBN 978 1 78521 085 3

Published by Haynes Publishing,
Sparkford, Yeovil, Somerset BA22 7JJ, UK
Tel: 01963 440635
Int. tel: +44 1963 440635
Website: www.haynes.co.uk

Haynes North America Inc.
861 Lawrence Drive, Newbury Park,
California 91320, USA

Printed and bound in the USA by Odcombe Press LP,
1299 Bridgestone Parkway, LaVergne, TN 37086

WOMEN'S HOME DIY

If you want something doing, do-it-yourself

Fix-it and Finish-it Manual

A multi-tasker's guide to home DIY, including
decorating, plumbing and electrics

Contents

INTRODUCTION 6

1 GETTING STARTED 8

Tools and kit	10
Using a drill	14
Using certain tools	16
Health and safety	18
Getting the Pros in	20

2 KNOW YOUR HOME 24

Electricity	26
Electricity circuits	28
Gas	30
Water	32
Heating	34
Greener home	36

3 DECORATING 38

Painting	40
Painting tools	44
Preparation	46
Cutting in	48
Cutting in	50
Woodwork	52
Wallpapering	56
Papering tools	58
Paper-hanging	60

4 FLOORING 64

Wooden Floors	66
Preparation	68
Laminate	70
Floor tiles	74
Vinyl flooring	78
Vinyl tiles	81

5 WINDOWS & DOORS 82

Curtain poles	84
Replacing glass	86
Fitting a door	88
Door handles	90
Window locks	92
Door locks	94

An excuse to shop. Buy your own toolkit

We're allowed to change our mind on the colour

8 OTHER DIY JOBS — 124

Shelving	126
Changing kitchen doors	128
Hanging a picture	130
Resealing bath and basin edges	132
Skirting boards	134
Fitting coving	136
Wall tiling	138
Replacing tiles	140

6 PLUMBING — 98

Leaking taps	100
Dishwashers & Washing Machines	103
Sinks & drains	106
Cisterns	108
Other problems	110

7 ELECTRICS — 112

Read this first	114
Fitting a plug	115
Socket covers	116
Light switches	118
Light fittings	120
Bright spark	122

9 SOLVING PROBLEMS — 142

Problems	144
Infestation	148
Heat loss	150
Fire prevention	152

GLOSSARY — 210

INDEX — 212

Introduction

Ten years ago, as I sat behind my desk dreamily looking out over the Thames and the skyline of the City of London from my office on the 14th floor of a glass skyscraper in Canary Wharf, little did I ever imagine that I'd be writing a Haynes Manual on DIY for women – and not just writing a book but also able to do everything described within it and more.

My journey from investment banker to fully fledged DIYer really began when I was a little girl, helping my Dad with his DIY around the house and holding the pieces of wood while he sawed them in two. Thanks to him I never developed a fear of anything practical – but don't worry if you do have a fear because it's very easy to overcome. I ended up taking a very conventional route through school, sixth form and university, and landed myself a cracking job in the City with a salary to match.

Suddenly, though, I found myself in a somewhat uncomfortable position with a lovely riverside apartment that needed renovating. Whereas I relished the chance to do it

The satisfaction of the demolition stage

myself, I didn't have the time as I was working all hours at the bank, but I could afford to pay someone else. I had to bite the bullet and 'get a man in'. Although it was a disastrous experience from beginning to end, I am actually very grateful to 'Dave' – as I shall call him even though I would dearly love to expose his identity. He helped to redirect my life by his dirty, unskilled work and his downright rudeness!

One day (or more likely very late one night) I returned from work in the hope of admiring my newly tiled kitchen floor, but I was struck dumb by the shocking sight of my beautiful apartment and belongings covered in a thick layer of white tile dust – it looked like it had snowed in my living room. 'Dave' had been cutting the tiles for my kitchen inside my living room, without covering any of my furniture with dust sheets, instead of the seemingly obvious alternative of working on the balcony. In fairness the balcony was two metres further from the kettle, which he used frequently judging by the numerous dirty cups he left strewn around the flat. When, on top of everything else, he tried to bully me into paying more than he'd originally quoted, I decided enough was enough. I was going to sort this out myself.

I had always hoped to set up my own business one day but had never known in what field. From that experience came my idea to set up a building company staffed by women. I would employ many tradeswomen, and base my enterprise on values and manners that I considered fundamental and basic, such as turning up on time, sticking to quoted prices, and treating someone's home as exactly that, rather than a building site. I called the company 'A Woman's Touch – Building and Construction' so that there could be no mistaking what we stood for and who we were.

A Woman's Touch grew strongly and within a few years my business employed 25 women and covered the whole of London and beyond, covering all the main trades as well as tackling projects such as bathrooms and kitchens. I myself learned more and more about the intricacies of various skills from tiling to plastering, plumbing to electrics, and even a spot of bricklaying, both through private courses and from working alongside skilled professionals.

We were very fortunate to receive a lot of awards for our work, and for being female pioneers in the field. I was even invited to a reception at Buckingham Palace for female entrepreneurs and met the Queen. I tried to submit a quote for some works I spotted needed doing on the Palace, but unfortunately I didn't hear from them on that! I did, however, manage to secure a contract working on a Gordon Ramsay restaurant at the Connaught hotel, and at the culmination of that project my team had to work through the night to ensure it could open for breakfast the next morning. A couple of years ago publicity in a well-known red-top paper popular on the Costa del Sol sparked interest from British residents there, so now I have expanded my business to Spain.

When Haynes approached me to write this book I jumped at the chance because the Women's Home DIY Manual will empower each and every woman to do DIY herself. From students making their tentative first steps away from home, to first-time buyers, housewives, mums and grannies, any woman whatsoever – with any kind of home whether owned or rented – can easily, cheaply, safely and effectively make repairs and improvements to their environment by following a few simple steps.

All you need to start is this book, a few simple tools, a willingness to give it a go and the belief that you can do it. We women have a knack of multi-tasking very well and should take advantage of this. We do not need to 'get a man in' (or a woman for that matter). We do not need to try to bully or cajole our other halves, dads or brothers to do these things for us. We have the power and aptitude, and now the knowledge, to crack on and do it ourselves.

So, come on ladies – the time has come. Put down this manual, pick up your tool kit and start the transformation of your home!

Kerrie Hanafin
Spring 2011

The team at A Woman's Touch, back in 2007

GETTING STARTED

DIY stands for Do It Yourself, of course – not Do It Himself. There's nothing about having a hairy chest and big feet that makes you any good at DIY, and don't believe anybody who tells you otherwise. Most DIY jobs are very straightforward once you know what you're up to, and armed with this book and a few tools you can tackle pretty much anything. There's something very satisfying about completing a major household job too. Sisters, as the song nearly says, should be doing it for themselves.

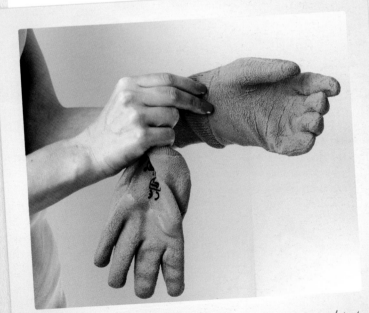

You may find some of the essential kit in your favourite colour

Tools and kit

The first thing you need is a tool kit. There are a few tools on the market specifically aimed at women, which tend to be lighter with slimmer handles – but don't fall for those gift sets of floral hammers and so on, as they're strictly for novelty purposes. However, with some careful shopping, you can find the perfect tool kit to suit you.

What you need

The list of essentials is fairly short and inexpensive. As you grow in confidence and ability, you will probably want to add to your collection, but below are the basic tools you'll need for general jobs around the house. Specific tools for more specialist jobs, such as decorating, will be listed in the relevant chapters later on.

Three screwdrivers

Two slotted-head (flat head) one for small screws and one for medium-large screws, and one Phillips screwdriver (cross head). The longer the handle, the more leverage you have for turning stubborn screws. Try to buy magnetic screwdrivers – which means you will drop less screws.

A claw hammer

The claw side is useful for removing nails and requires a lot less brute force than using a pair of conventional pliers.

Let the hammer do the hard work

Pencils, note pad and straight ruler

Make sure the ruler is metal rather than wood or plastic so that you can use it to cut along.

Tape measure

Ideally a metal retractable type. Make sure it has a thumb stop as well as showing both metric and imperial measurements.

Spirit level

Ideally a metre long, but smaller ones can also work well, and ensure that it has both horizontal and vertical vials (the glass bits with the bubble in).

Allen keys

Buy a set of different size and shape allen keys on a key ring. Flat pack furniture manufacturers usually provide one with each purchase, but rather than having lots of single ones rattling around your tool box and getting lost, a set on a ring is the safest option.

Pliers

There are three types of pliers as shown, although I would also suggest buying combination pliers which offer the same functionality in one tool, ie gripping (including small items such as electrical wires) and also cutting.

Bradawls

Pointed screwdriver-type things for making holes – often look old-fashioned and remind you of the toy maker from *Pinocchio*, but are an absolute god-send when it comes to drilling.

Chisel

The chisel should be bevel-edged and have a protective guard.

Craft knife

More commonly known as a Stanley knife.

Adjustable spanner

Easier than keeping a set of spanners.

Hacksaw

Junior hacksaw (right) for cutting plastic trim. Larger hacksaw for bigger tasks.

The tool box

The first thing you'll need is a suitable container to keep your tools in. Most tool boxes on the market are so large and hefty that when full they are ridiculously heavy and impractical to cart around – but using a bit of cleverness you can create a perfect, portable toolkit to suit you. Look around for plastic ones, or the more lightweight metal type. It should have at least one internal tray with dividers, where you can store smaller, lighter tools such as screwdrivers, and a deeper section below for large items such as hammers. If possible buy a tool box that also has a further divider tray to store tiny bits like screws, wall plugs and nails in order of size so they're instantly accessible.

Pull out internal tray

Kerrie's top tip

Look for a tool box with built-in wheels, like the hand luggage bags you take on a plane. That way, even when it's full of tools, it won't be too difficult to manoeuvre around.

Wheely good!

Plasterboard Saw

This saw is designed specifically for cutting dry wall panels and plasterboard.

String

Always useful to have close at hand.

Masking tape

Protects adjoining areas when working.

Electrical tape

For colour coding wires when working with electrics.

Assortment of wall fixings

Screws, nails and wall plugs – the most well-known are Rawlplugs – for solid and hollow walls. Mixed packs are available in DIY stores which contain a variety of all of the above, and these are a great starting point.

Drill and bits

There are thousands of drills on the market, but I suggest a mid range, cordless drill with two speeds and which comes with assorted drill bits (suitable for masonry, plasterboard, wood, tiles and so on – these will be described in more detail in the relevant chapters later on). If drilling regularly into masonry walls or floors then one with a hammer function is a good idea. The lower speed option will be useful for tiles, glass and metal, whilst the higher speed is best for wood and walls. Later you can add other accessories such as sanding discs. The main thing at this stage is that it feels comfortable in your hand and that you can hold it tightly enough to apply pressure when necessary. The guys in the DIY store will think you are slightly unhinged when you ask to hold the drill to test it for size, but this is really important for women as we tend to have smaller hands than the men these tools are designed for.

Wire and pipe locator

This is a small gadget normally called a stud finder or metal detector, and it is invaluable as it will let you know if there are any wires or metal pipes in the area you are about to drill. They are not expensive, and worth every penny compared to the possible consequences of drilling through a pipe or cable.

Dust sheets and cloths

There is no need to buy dust sheets, we all have suitable items lying around the home such as old curtains, bed sheets, old shower curtains and even flattened cardboard boxes. Using plenty of these in the first place will save you enormous headaches later when it comes to cleaning up.

Stepladder

The two main criteria you should consider for a ladder are height (ensure it allows you to comfortably reach the ceiling of your home), and weight – the lighter it is, the easier it is to carry around. Make sure it's sturdy, though.

Ladder safety

When you are working on a ladder or scaffold you need to be extra cautious about your balance and footing. Never over-extend yourself just to reach that extra few centimetres, instead go back down the ladder, move it along, then climb up again. If you are using a stepladder, ensure that it is securely clicked into place before climbing up. If you are on a standard ladder make sure it's correctly assembled and check the angle between the ladder, floor and wall. If you've got someone else to help, get them to stand at the bottom with their foot on the bottom rung to give it extra stability. Always leave one hand free to hold the ladder, and make sure you can't drop anything such as unsecured tins of paint or tools on to people below.

✔ Step in good condition

✔ Right height for the job no overreaching

✔ Good grip 3 points of contact

✔ Front towards work

✔ Correct flat shoes

✔ Clean treads

✔ Four feet in good condition

✔ Firm on level base

Using a drill

This is something that most women seem to be frightened of initially, but trust me, there really is no need. So long as you've checked the wall with your detector so you're not going to drill through any wires or pipes, and you follow the guidelines below, you'll be putting up shelves and installing curtain poles in no time.

How to drill

As a rule make sure you, and the thing you are drilling, are secure and grounded (ie don't be wobbling at the top of an unstable ladder) and if it isn't a cordless drill, ensure the cable is well out of the way. Hold the drill at a right angle to the surface you are drilling. It helps if you make a little dent or guide hole with your bradawl first to give your drill bit something to guide it in for the first few millimetres. Pick your drill bit according to the surface you are drilling into, and according to the size of the hole you require – be guided by the size of the wall plug rather than the screw.

Whilst drilling, keep the speed steady and pull the drill back out again every few seconds to allow the waste to fall out of the hole. You should never have to push too hard to drill. However, if the drill slows down or the noise of the motor reduces the drill is overworking, so allow it to rest for a minute before continuing or it might overheat.

10mm Keyless chuck. Some older drills use Keyed chucks

Torque control collar with hammer function

Soft grip variable speed switch

Keyed chuck with Key

14.4V removable battery. Comes with charger

14.4V

Wall plugs

Or as they're also known – Rawlplugs. Make sure you use the correct type for the wall. Stud walls need the ones with the 'arms' so they grip onto the plasterboard.

Wood bit
A wood bit has a point for accurate positioning and a sharp cutting thread.

Most drills come with a double ended screwdriver bit attached to the side

Masonry bit
A masonry bit has a tungsten-carbide tip and should be used for drilling concrete, stone, bricks and plaster.

Typical weights of cordless drills are 2–3kg

Forward/ reverse switch

Metal bit
A metal bit has a v-shaped tip and is made from steel. Use it for drilling metal but it can also be used for wood.

Corded vs Cordless

I've recommended a cordless drill as it's easy to transport and tends to be lighter, but corded drills are also excellent, and can be especially useful if you are drilling into very hard surfaces such as bricks or blockwork, as they tend to have more power than battery operated cordless drills, and obviously can keep going without needing to be recharged.

Countersink bit
A countersink bit has a wide pointed end. It is used to make the ideal shape for countersinking screw heads in wood so they lay flush with the surface.

Flat wood bit
A flat wood bit is used to drill large holes in wood.

Using certain tools

We'll look at most tools in the relevant sections later on in the book – however, here are a couple of general pointers on the less obvious (or more scary) items in your shiny new toolkit. If you're uncertain, it's a good idea to practise on some spare wood to start with.

Chisel

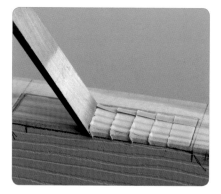

These have to be very sharp to be good at their job – cutting lumps out of wood – so you need to be careful. Take your time and go steady. There are two ways to use a chisel; the first simply with hand pressure for smaller jobs, the second by hitting the handle with a mallet to make deeper cuts into a piece of wood. The most likely method that you'll use is the former, for jobs such as removing small areas of rotten wood from a door or frame, or making a space to fix a door hinge. Both of your hands should be behind the blade at all times and the bevel – the slanted part of the blade – needs to face away from the edge of the wood. Use your main hand (ie right if you're right handed) to hold the handle and exert pressure, and your other hand just to guide the blade and remove small slivers of wood.

Chisels are often used with a wooden mallet

Hammer

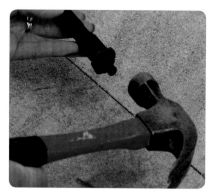

You will grow in confidence very quickly once you start using a hammer. Let's use the example of hammering in a nail into a piece of wood. Start by holding the nail in place between your thumb and index finger. Gently hit the head of the nail with the hammer a few times until the nail has sunk into the wood enough to hold it in place, so that you can stop holding it with your other hand. Doing this gently means that if you do miss (but you won't!) then you won't whack your hand, or the surrounding wood. Once the nail is held in place, you can let rip a little more on the force side, and hit the nail more firmly, repeating until it is all the way down and the head is flush with the wood. Be careful to hit the nail straight as otherwise you can bend it. If this does happen, just use the claw part of the hammer to remove the nail, and start again with a new one.

Saw

The key here is actually the material you are sawing. Make sure it is securely held in place and won't slip, either by holding it down with your other hand over the edge of a table or work bench, or clamped in place leaving your other hand free. It is vital it is over the edge of the surface, otherwise you'll be sawing through your table or work bench too! Start by drawing the saw gently across the corner of the wood (or whatever you're cutting), along the line you've marked in pencil, a few times so that you make a small indent. This can now be used to guide your blade and stop the saw from moving around from side to side. Continue sawing in longer, smoother movements all the way until you are almost finished, and then for the very last section use shorter, softer strokes again. Be ready to catch the piece you're cutting off, or have the floor protected underneath if you're going to let it fall down.

Screwdriver

Firstly you need to pick the right head for the screw you are using (flat head or Phillips) and also the right size. Then simply push the screw driver into the end of the screw and push as you twist clockwise to tighten a screw. To untighten or remove a screw, turn anticlockwise, but you still have to push to maintain good contact. A good phrase to remember is 'righty tighty, lefty loosey' – to remind you which way to turn the screw driver!

Spanner

Spanners are used to tighten or loosen nuts. If you have an adjustable spanner, start by placing the gripper part over the top of the nut and twist the wheel until the jaws tighten around the flat sides of the nut. Ideally hold it horizontally to the nut to maintain better contact, rather than coming at it from above, but sometimes this isn't possible depending where the nut is. Then follow the same guidelines for tightening and loosening screws in terms of which direction to turn the spanner.

Craft knife

Obviously these have very sharp blades, so it is advisable to always cut in a direction away from you in case you slip. Hold the knife relatively flat (not upright) to cut and slide it along. Ensure the blade is always sharp and change it when necessary (spares are stored inside the body of the blade and can be accessed by unscrewing the casing) to avoid tearing/snagging the thing you are cutting.

Plane

Use this for shaving wood down to size. Press the blade firmly against the timber and run it along the length, pushing down on the knob at the front. Repeat the process until you have shaved off enough wood. It's important to set the angle of the blade correctly so it doesn't dig into the wood. Make sure you keep the blade sharp and at the correct angle. Practise on a spare piece of wood first.

When to hire or buy

The general rule about hiring equipment is that if you're going to use it more than three times it's probably worth buying. For example, if you've moved into a new house and want to sand down the floors, one room at a time, it is going to be more cost effective to buy a floor sander than to hire one on several occasions. If you do hire equipment, remember to factor in the cost of extras such as sandpaper, circuit breakers, and health and safety equipment which are normally added to the hire price. Make sure you always return the equipment on time to avoid costly fines.

Kerrie's top tip

If you are planning on doing a lot of work and hiring various different tools, then it is a good idea to set up an account with a hire firm, who may well offer reduced rates, free delivery and collection, which can save you valuable time as well as money.

Health and safety

I can't cover every possible bit of information in this section, otherwise it would be a manual on its own. There's only one basic thing you need – common sense. Trust your intuition. Does something feel wobbly, unsafe or unwise? Stop. Have a think. If it feels dodgy, it probably is. Read up on your job before you start – particularly the safety instructions on any products you use. Follow them – they're there to stop you doing something silly.

Protective equipment

Here are some basic personal protection items which you should have for your DIY work. Yes, some aren't terribly flattering or fashionable, but a big splash of emulsion in the eye is so not a good look this season.

Multi-tasking – safety and a steam facial

Goggles
Protective plastic goggles protect your eyes from any flying pieces of debris or splashes. These should always be worn when drilling, chiselling, or using toxic substances. Safety glasses are less restrictive, and if they fit snugly they will do for lighter jobs.

Face masks
These should be worn when drilling or sanding, or when particles or fumes are being created. There are various different masks on the market depending on the task in hand. You should be especially cautious if you are pregnant or trying to get pregnant – always seek the advice of your doctor.

Gloves
These are highly recommended for certain tasks and essential for others. Disposable plastic gloves are useful for decorating (white spirit plays havoc with nail varnish and dries out the skin in seconds), and for other tasks you might need more solid leather or heatproof gloves.

Overalls

These are great for protecting your clothes from dirt and paint – and they also provide useful pockets for tools to save you trips up and down a step ladder. A good, cheap alternative is an old shirt with a breast pocket.

Footwear

This is also an important consideration. If you are working in an environment where you could drop something heavy, steel toe capped shoes or boots are ideal. There are several internet sites offering these in women's sizes and less heavy versions than the traditional male clod-hoppers, although they still have a long way to go before they could be classed as a style rival to killer heels.

Ditch the killer heels for the day

Long hair

Not an issue for most men, but can be dangerous for the female DIYer, so make sure it is tied back securely so that it can't get in your eyes or get caught in anything. If in doubt stick a cap on over the top just to make sure – and this will also prevent paint spatters making you look like you have a bad case of dandruff.

Hazards

DIY will put you in some situations involving potential hazards which you may not come across in your normal day-to-day life, so always take a few minutes before you start to assess the situation. There's no need to be scared – but be prepared. Remember that your worst enemy is rushing, panicking or flapping. Keep a cool head and take your time.

✳ Trip hazards

These include trailing cables, dust sheets, tools, even helpers or pets! Just be sensible and keep your working environment clean and tidy to minimise this risk. Run cables around edges of rooms where possible, or tape them down to floors.

✳ Electricity

This is a specialist area and there are very stringent rules in place preventing DIYers from putting themselves and others in danger. Do not overload plug sockets, visually check the cables of any tools you are using to make sure they aren't damaged in any way and make sure you know where cables run through walls you may be working on so that you don't drill into them by accident. It's always a good idea to turn off the electricity at the main fusebox before you start electrical work.

✳ Toxic substances

Many DIY products can be harmful to your health and/or the environment if not used properly. Make sure you read the label carefully so that you understand the precautions you should take in terms of ventilation and protective equipment, and also how to dispose of them properly so you don't harm the environment.

✳ Fire

If you are working with flammable materials, or naked flames such as a blowtorch or other heat source, be particularly careful. A small multi-purpose fire extinguisher is a good idea, and also make sure you don't block your or other people's escape routes with tools or rubbish.

Getting the Pros in

This book is about empowering us to do it for ourselves, and not having to pull in favours from husbands, brothers, dads, uncles and mates – or even parting with our hard-earned cash to pay someone else to do it for us.

However, there are some jobs which must be left to a professional, and others which you might prefer to leave to an expert. So this section should help you choose the best person for the job, demystify some of the terms they'll use, and give you advance warning of the prices they'll charge. Here are a few handy points to watch out for:

* While the prices opposite are daily rates, do your best to get a fixed quote for the whole job before committing to a price.
* Whoever you choose to use, be prepared to do a little shopping around and meet two or three potential workers before making your choice.
* Always ask for a written quote and ensure everything is included, including materials.
* Don't always go for the cheapest option – you normally get what you pay for.
* Be guided by recommendations from friends and family, and ask for references or examples of their previous work.

You could learn a skill and become a pro (see www.wamt.org)

Kerrie's top tip

Remember there are now many handywomen and female tradespeople out there, so if you prefer to have another woman working in your house, you now have that choice in most areas of the country. Try www.awomanstouch.org.uk or www.wamt.org.

* You may be able to save money by doing some of the ground work or preparation yourself. They may also be willing to let you help, or at least watch and learn how they do what they do. A good tradesperson is usually delighted to share their knowledge with their clients, but make sure you don't get in their way and slow them down.
* Who will buy the materials? Many tradespeople or professional companies can get trade discounts from the suppliers, and if this is the case it may well be the most cost-effective option for you so long as they pass some of this discount on to you, so double-check before agreeing to their quote. If you are going to buy your own materials, don't be afraid to ask the professionals for advice on quantities and brands.
* Finally, make sure any quote you receive includes a clean up, which whilst it may not be up to your exacting standards, should at least be a good start and should include removing any rubbish they have generated from your home.

Painter/decorator

This is the trade which is often considered the easiest, but once you have given it a go for yourself you will quickly come to appreciate that it is a skilled profession. A good decorator will spend a large proportion of the time preparing the surfaces and only a small amount of time actually applying the paint finishes. A regular painter and decorator should charge around £100–£150 a day, a more specialist painter used for papering or specialist paint effects can charge up to £400 a day. Bear in mind that you can often save a lot of money by doing basic preparation yourself, and just using the professional right at the end for the parts you find too tricky.

Plasterer

This is usually a team effort, as plasterers find it's more efficient to have someone helping them (a labourer) to mix up the plaster and speed up the process, so make sure your quote includes both people. This is likely to be £200–£300 a day for the two. There are two options for plastering walls and ceilings – wet plaster which dries pink and smooth and is then painted onto (ensure it is fully dry first, otherwise you can cause it to crack), or dry lining, which is when plasterboard sheets are screwed onto the joists (or sometimes stuck on using a technique called 'dot and dab'), and the joins are then taped over with scrim tape and filled so they are smooth and ready for painting. Plastering tends to be a very messy, dusty process, so make sure your chosen professional masks up their working area well to avoid damage to surrounding areas.

Tiler

Tiling professionally is a truly skilled profession. Some tiles are relatively easy to work with (standard size, ceramic tiles), whilst others are rather tricky (mosaic or very large tiles, and those made from glass or marble), so your choice of DIY or professional may well be dictated by your choice of tile. A tiler should charge around £150–£200 a day, depending on the type of tiles and the difficulty of the shapes and surfaces to be tiled. Tiling is also a messy business, both in mixing the grout and adhesive and cutting the tiles, so ideally make sure your tiler has access to an outside space where dust doesn't matter, or alternatively ensure they mask up the area they are working on thoroughly. If your work is just a small splashback for a sink, then it is most likely something you could tackle yourself.

Carpenter

These guys and girls tend to be multi-skilled and can do general carpentry work such as skirting boards, doors, floors, to more specialist 'joiner' work such as building kitchens or making built-in cupboards and door frames. They are often called 'chippies' and vary in cost from £150–£250 per day depending on how specialised the work is. A consideration for carpenters is that they'll require a large working space for their tools and materials.

Plumber/Gas fitter

Generally, plumbers deal with water (bathrooms, kitchens, toilets, drainage) while gas fitters deal with the gas installations in your house (central heating boiler, gas fire, gas hob). By law you are not allowed to deal with any gas installations yourself – it is essential that you use a Gas Safe registered professional – and do check their credentials online at www.gassaferegister.co.uk before giving them the job. You will be given a certificate after the works to prove that they have been carried out by a Gas Safe operative and you will need to keep this for insurance purposes or if you are planning to sell your house. A Gas Safe plumber will cost around £150–£250 a day. When it comes to water, you have a lot more leeway and are free to undertake works yourself, but if you do get out of your depth (oops) a plumber should cost £100–£200 a day.

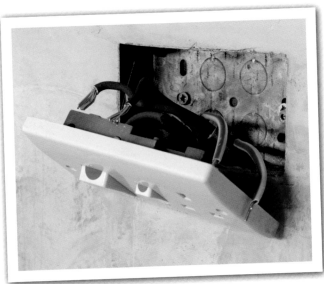

Electrician

There are now stringent laws governing working with electrics in the home. NICEIC and similar bodies test and certify electricians, who are then entitled to work on new and existing electrical installations within the home. There are strict guidelines governing size of wires, location of switches in relation to taps and water, loading of various circuits and so on. You will receive a certificate following any new works which will include a test of the existing circuits in the house and highlight any problems there may be. This will also be needed should you wish to sell your house so is worth keeping, and do act on any advice regarding repairs and upgrades needed. Electricians should charge £150–£250 a day, and may well charge extra for the certification – so make sure you ask for this to be itemised at the quote stage.

Glazier

A glazier should charge £100–£200 a day and can carry out any tasks involving glass, from windows and doors to shower screens and more adventurous installations. In most cases, you should be able to undertake simple repairs yourself, but for more complicated panes of glass, or where specialist cutting is required, you may be better off using a professional. An alternative is to ask a glazier to cut the glass for you, but to install it yourself.

Handywoman

This is a catch all term for a generally experienced individual, though be cautious as they may not be qualified in any particular trade. That said, they can be extremely useful for a variety of smaller tasks, and are likely to charge a lower overall amount than individual tradespeople would for doing a mixture of jobs. A handyperson should charge between £100–£200 a day depending on their skill level, however unlike other tradespeople it is most likely that you will need to supply all necessary materials.

Builder

This is another generic term which can mean a variety of things, but on the whole a builder is able to deal with larger jobs such as building an extension, doing a loft conversion or knocking through walls and installing internal structural supports. They are likely to be able to recommend other professionals to you, such as architects and structural engineers, who you may need to involve in larger projects, and they may also be able to guide you through the process of obtaining permission for your planned works. Builders can cost between £150–£250 a day, but are the most likely of all the trades to work on a total project cost rather than a daily rate.

COMPL

MK

LN 5500 s

100A AC22A

MAIN
SWITCH

N1 ⌐ L1
N2 L2

MK

LN 5932 s
B 32
240V∼
6000

MK

LN 5932 s
B 32
240V∼
6000
3

0 · OFF

MK

LN 5916 s
B 16
240V∼
6000

LN
B
24
60

I · ON

I · ON

COOKER

WATER
HEATER

B
H

KNOW YOUR HOME

This is probably the most important chapter in the whole manual. Even if you've got no intention of ever picking up a tool and doing any DIY, understanding how your home works can keep you safe, save you money, and even help the environment. So here's where I'll tell you about the services that come into your home – electricity, gas and water – and how to deal with them and their potential problems. We will also look at heating in some detail, including exploring the different options available to you, and the pros and cons of each.

Hot water and heating – no girl can live without it

Electricity

I'm going to guide you through the electricity in your home from the outside in, starting with the big stuff and ending up with individual lights and sockets. So here's a simple explanation of how things work and how they fit together.

A modern home has a wealth of electrics from extractors to underfloor heating

Your home will be connected to the national electricity network via underground or high-level cables. Its first stop when it reaches you is an electricity company-owned sealed fuse. It then flows through your meter, and into your fuse box – now often called an 'electricity consumer unit'. The fuse and meter are normally mounted on a meter board in a meter cupboard outside or just inside your property, and both belong to the electricity company. It's actually illegal to tamper with them yourself or to break the seals.

Electricity meter

The meter measures the amount of electricity you use (in units) and your electricity supplier will charge you at a set rate per unit based on this usage. You can arrange to provide your own regular meter readings so that they can bill you accurately rather than them making estimates, then balancing up by taking an annual meter reading. It is also possible to switch to an Economy 7 tariff – where you pay less for electricity used in the evenings and overnight, but a higher rate during the day. This could save you a great deal of money, so it is worth talking to your provider to decide what would suit your usage best.

When you move into a new home (whether you are renting or whether you own it), always take meter readings to make sure you're not being charged for the previous tenant's or owner's usage.

There are different types of meter, all performing exactly the same function. A dial meter has clock-like dials, where you read from left to right, but ignore the red dial. If the pointer is in-between two numbers, take the lower number. Another style is like the one shown, where you just read across the single row (or double row if you have two rates).

The more modern electronic style has a digital display, as shown on the right.

You can check out www.edfenergy.com where you can find detailed instructions.

The fuse box

This is the point where the electricity company's responsibility ends and yours starts. A fuse box, or fuse board is now more commonly called a consumer unit, which emphasises the division of responsibility at this point. The consumer unit receives electricity from the electricity company's sealed fuse in the meter cupboard, via the meter. The consumer unit splits up the different circuits that run around your home (explored in more detail in the next section) and each of these has its own fuse, or circuit breaker.

Older style consumer units, like the one on the right, have rewirable or cartridge type fuses. If there is a problem on the circuit, the fuse will blow, thus protecting the problem section from overheating and catching fire. There is also a mains switch which cuts off or restores the electricity supply to the house.

Newer consumer units do not have fuses; instead they have miniature circuit breakers which switch themselves off if there is a problem, or if the circuit is overloaded. These often work in the opposite direction to normal UK switches – up for on, down for off. But they should also be clearly labelled. And as with the older style unit there is also usually a main switch, or a master switch for several circuits.

If you, or any tradespeople, are working on any electrical items, or unscrewing switches or plug sockets for any reason (such as

decorating) then it is essential that the electricity supply to that area is switched off. On a new consumer unit, each circuit should be labelled, so for example 'upstairs lights' can be switched off whilst the rest of the house remains live. On an older unit, you will need to turn everything off at once. But if in doubt, turn everything off.

If you have recently moved, or if your system has not been inspected for several years, then it is highly advisable to arrange for an electrician to come and test each of your circuits and certify them as safe. This can save your home, and even your life, so is money well spent. It could also reduce your insurance premiums.

Know your switches

In this consumer unit, the main switch (on the left) is used to isolate all electrical circuits in the house. The middle part of the unit houses the miniature circuit breakers (MCB) which protect the individual circuits in the house. Each of these is rated according to the load on the circuit – you can see the ratings on each MCB. On the right of the consumer unit is the Residual Current Device (RCD) which offers protection in the event of an earth fault. If a fault does occur, the RCD quickly shuts off the supply, reducing the risk of death or serious injury. The operation of the RCD should be checked at least once a year by pressing the test button.

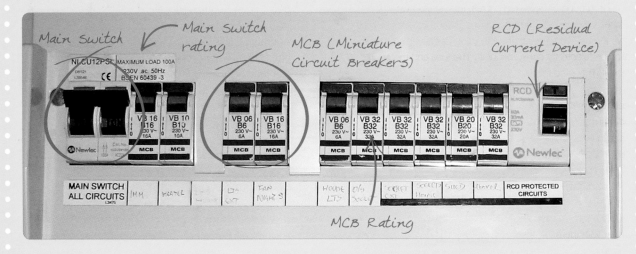

Electricity circuits

What comes out of the consumer unit? At first glance all those switches look complicated, but read this and take a closer look at them and all will become clear. It will also help if you're going to have a go at any of the jobs involving electrics in Chapter seven.

Lighting circuit(s)

This is the circuit which, unsurprisingly, supplies power to the lights in your home. The amount of current running through this circuit is low (5 amps) because the power requirement (wattage) of lights is low. The wire supplying the power runs from the consumer unit to the first rose in the circuit. The rose is the white plastic ceiling fixture on a standard light fitting. In modern homes there should also be another wire running on to the next rose, and so on until the last one in the circuit is reached. In older homes, all roses will feed off a central junction box located in the ceiling. Most houses will have two lighting circuits, maybe more, and each circuit will service around 8 to 10 lights.

In addition to the wires running to the rose and between the roses, there is another wire which runs from each rose, across the ceiling and down the wall to the light switch which enables the light to be turned on and off. However – and this is a very important point – the light switch does not stop power going to the rose, as it is connected directly to the consumer unit, so turn the power off before you unscrew the rose fitting, by ensuring the lighting circuit is turned off at the consumer unit. You can check this by leaving the light turned on, flicking the switch in the consumer unit to 'off', then returning to check that the light is no longer lit.

Knowing that these wires exist, and where they run, is crucial in DIY so you can avoid accidentally drilling through a cable or

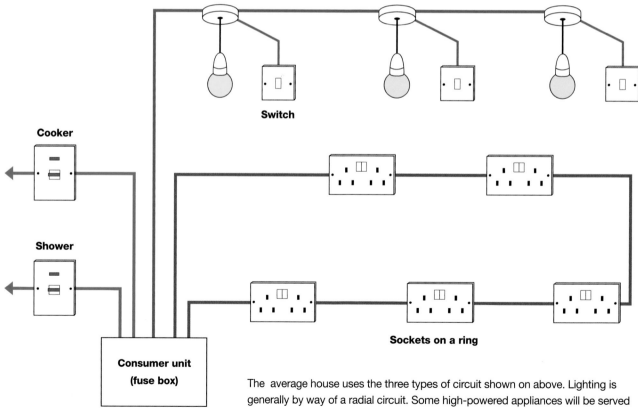

Radial lighting circuit

Switch

Cooker

Shower

Consumer unit (fuse box)

Sockets on a ring

The average house uses the three types of circuit shown on above. Lighting is generally by way of a radial circuit. Some high-powered appliances will be served by individual radial circuits, while sockets are fed from a ring main arrangement. This illustration is greatly simplified, but shows how the various circuits differ.

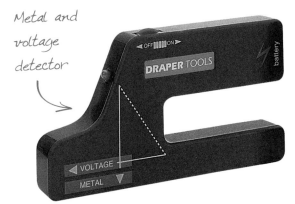

Metal and voltage detector

hammering a nail into one. Use your cable detector (described in the 'your toolkit' section of the first chapter) to check their location before starting any work. Cables normally run straight up or down vertically and sometimes horizontally from switches and sockets – but don't rely on this, as it entirely depends on the quality of the electrician who installed the wires in the first place. I've come across many incredibly dangerous examples of hidden wires haphazardly trailing diagonally across walls.

Ring circuit (sockets)

This circuit supplies power to sockets and appliances, and is called a ring circuit because it forms a complete loop, ending up back in the consumer unit having run from socket to socket. As with lighting circuits, the average home will have two ring circuits, one upstairs and one downstairs. The cable runs from the consumer unit to the first socket and from that one to the next and so on, with the cable from the last socket leading back to the consumer unit. Occasionally there may be a spur cable – this means another cable running off a socket to provide extra sockets, in addition to the main loop.

The power requirement of appliances using sockets is higher than lights; therefore the total power supply (wattage) in this circuit is higher, so the current running through the circuit is higher, at 30 amps. This is the circuit which provides power to your TV, microwave, dishwasher, washing machine, hairdryer, fridge, computer and so on. But not your cooker – that should be on a separate radial circuit (see below) as it has a very high power demand on its own. Some of your appliances may be wired directly into the circuit via an isolator switch, rather than a conventional three-pin plug. This is for safety, and also convenience so the individual appliance can be isolated from the circuit to be worked on, rather than having to turn everything off.

Radial circuit (high wattage)

The radial circuit is a special circuit which supplies power to high-powered equipment such as cookers. The power supply is likely to be the same as the ring circuit, 30 amps, but can be higher – for example for a larger cooker it would be 45 amps. The cooker should have its own control unit, which is effectively an isolator switch for that appliance. High-wattage appliances have their own circuit for safety, so they don't overload the main ring circuit.

Electricity Terminology

We've mentioned these terms briefly, but for clarity here's a quick guide.

✳ Watts
This is the power required by an appliance. Your cooker may need up to around 4,000 watts (also known as 4 kilowatts). Watts are what you pay for – they are what your electricity meter measures.

✳ Volts
This is the pressure that drives the power through the wires. In the UK it is 240V, and in the USA it is 110V. But it's not completely stable – it can drop if there is a surge in demand at a particular time (like the commercial break in the middle of *Coronation Street*). If this happens you may notice the picture on the television shrinks, fluorescent lights may flicker or refuse to work and the kettle will take ages to boil.

✳ Amps
This is the amount of current flowing through the circuit. The more power an appliance requires, the more amps the circuit needs to provide. Fuses are measured in amps (see below).

✳ Fuse
This is a weak point which is deliberately inserted into each circuit as a safety precaution. The fuse will blow if there is an overload. Plugs attached to appliances requiring less than 750 watts will generally have a 3 amp fuse, while equipment requiring more than 750 watts will need a 15 amp fuse. There are also fuses in older consumer units – 5 amps for the lighting circuit, 15 amps for an immersion heater, 30 amps for ring circuits and normal cookers, and 45 amps for large cookers.

Always keep some spare fuses

Gas

Not all homes have a mains gas feed, but in urban areas, most houses and many flats do. Most things to do with gas are not DIY jobs, but it's good to know the basics, and what to do in case of problems.

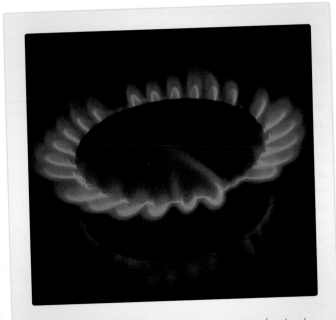

Get your appliances regularly checked by a Gas Safe registered engineer

Gas meter

Your gas meter will most likely be located in a meter cupboard or possibly under the stairs. Some will be like an old style electricity meter, reading the dials from left to right. Others will look like the one below.

A safe gas appliance

A well-maintained appliance will have a blue flame. Ventilation grilles or air bricks will be kept clear and external flues won't be blocked or covered.

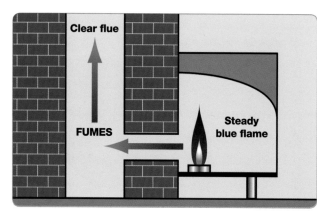

A dangerous gas appliance

If there is a yellow or orange flame (except for fuel-effect fires) or soot or stains around the appliance, turn it off immediately and get it checked by a Gas Safe registered engineer.

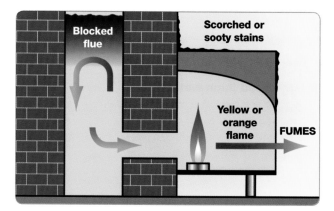

Avoid gas problems

Of all the three main services, gas has the most stringent laws as to who is allowed to do what. The rule is, basically, that you're not allowed to install or service any gas burning equipment yourself – you must use a Gas Safe registered fitter. You can find one, or check the credentials of an existing fitter on the website www.gassaferegister.co.uk. You might have heard of the Corgi scheme – Gas Safe replaced it on 1st April 2009.

However, there are certainly things you can do to make your home safer, and to prepare just in case there is a problem.

✳ Find your mains gas tap, make sure it works

The gas tap is usually found near your gas meter. If the handle is in line with the pipe it is on and if the handle is at a 90 degree angle to the pipe, it is off (see photo below). Check the handle to see if it is stiff, if it is then call your gas supplier, never try to force it or to fix it yourself.

✳ Turn it down and take a safe break

Some books suggest that you turn off your gas supply if you are going away on a long holiday. I would instead suggest turning your thermostat right down but not turning the heating off completely in winter, otherwise you could return to frozen or burst pipes.

✳ Avoid dangerous fumes

If fumes do escape they can be harmful to your health, and carbon monoxide poisoning can be fatal. Take sensible precautions to avoid fumes polluting your home – have your chimney swept before you have an appliance fitted, never block a ventilator, have appliances serviced regularly by a certified Gas Safe fitter and look out for tell-tale signs on malfunctioning appliances such as the pilot light continually blowing out, an orange or yellow flame instead of a blue one, a brown or black scorched area on an appliance, a musty smell or signs of soot, or more condensation than normal on your windows.

✳ What if you smell gas?

If you think there might be a leak, take immediate action. Extinguish any naked flames or candles, open all windows to let fresh air in, turn off all gas appliances and if possible turn off your mains gas tap. Immediately call National Grid Gas Emergencies (which used to be Transco) on 0800 111 999. Do not turn any electrical switches on or off, in case they cause a spark.

Carbon monoxide

Carbon monoxide (CO) is a highly poisonous, colourless, odourless and tasteless gas which is produced during incomplete combustion of gas and other fuels. This happens when a gas appliance has been incorrectly fitted or repaired or hasn't been maintained properly. It can also occur if flues, chimneys or vents are blocked. Oil and solid fuels can also produce carbon monoxide.

Carbon monoxide poisoning symptoms can be similar to flu, food poisoning, viral infections and general tiredness. It's therefore vital to be aware of these similarities, especiallly if you notice them only occuring when you are in your home and when other people (and pets) in the household are also suffering. The six main symptoms to look out for are headaches, dizziness, nausea, breathlessness, collapsing and loss of consciousness. If you suspect carbon monoxide poisoning, get fresh air immediately, turn off gas appliances and seek immediate medical attention (a blood or breath test can confirm if it's poisoning).

Get a Gas Safe registered engineer to inspect your gas appliances and flues. It literally could save lives.

Consider installing a carbon monoxide detector. These are very reasonably priced, widely available at DIY stores, easy to fit to the wall – and could save your life. The label should display BS 7860 in Britain, showing it is officially approved. Just as with a smoke detector, you should test your detector every month and replace batteries when necessary.

Water

Water is the service you are most likely to be involved with in your DIY projects, so it's important to understand how it gets into and around your home. In Chapter six I'll look at some of the more common water-related tasks you may want to have a go at, but here I'll just explain how the water gets into and around your home and what to do when things go wrong.

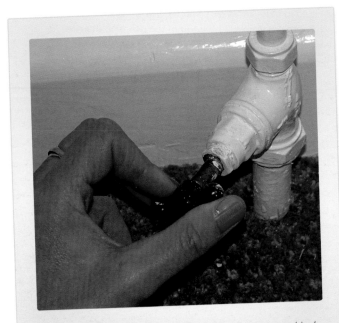

Know where your stop cock is and that you can turn it on and off easily

Water meter

Most homes in the UK are charged a fixed amount for their water services, which covers the delivery of fresh, clean water to the home, and the removal of waste water and sewage from the home. In recent years, though, more and more homes are being switched over to water meters where the quantities of water used and removed are measured, and the householder charged accordingly. I think this is a positive development; it will encourage homes to be more economical with their usage, and also even out the balance between moderate users and extreme ones – for example those with swimming pools.

www.apolloflow.co.uk

The water comes into your house via water mains which run under the road. From here a service pipe runs to the water supplier's stopcock (a heavy-duty tap), and everything up to this point is the responsibility of the water company. The water supplier's stopcock is located in an inspection chamber that will be near the house. From here, the service pipe becomes your responsibility and continues into your home, to another stopcock which can be used to stop the feed into the house. This main inlet pipe is often known as the rising main. In most houses, the rising main and stop cock will be found below or near to the kitchen sink.

Some homes have an indirect plumbing system, whereby the pipe then runs to a cold water cistern (or tank) normally in the loft, which in turn feeds the hot water cylinder, taps and cistern in the bathroom. The cold water tap in the kitchen should always be a direct offshoot from the main supply, ensuring the quality of water is suitable for drinking.

You may find that you have a direct plumbing system, where all cold taps are supplied directly at mains pressure, with the hot water system fed indirectly from a tank in the loft.

You can check which system you have by turning off the stop cock and turning on each tap in turn. If the tap keeps running, it is fed indirectly. If it dribbles to a stop after a few seconds, it is fed directly.

Just to confuse matters, there are variations of the two systems. In some cases you may find that you have a direct system, but that both bath taps are fed indirectly. This is to maintain equal pressure to each – important where a shower is fitted.

Avoid water problems

✳ Find and test your valves and stopcocks

Find them, label them if necessary, and test that you can turn them on and off. Do this once a year to avoid them seizing up. It is also common for water to weep around the spindle of the stop cock when it is disturbed. If this happens, try tightening the gland nut (the hexagon nearest the handle) a little. Don't overdo it though, or you won't be able to turn the stopcock on or off!

✳ Check your cold water cistern in the loft

Make sure it has a lid which fits but isn't completely airtight. On old metal cisterns, check for signs of corrosion inside and outside the cistern. Lagging the cold water pipes around the cistern will help prevent them from freezing; make sure you do the overflow pipe as well. However, do not lag underneath the tank as that will cut it off from the house's heat and you may end up with a frozen tank in winter.

✳ Check your washing machine pipes

Sometimes the pipes can split or work loose. It's much easier to deal with this before something goes wrong than to deal with the consequences if they come off during a wash cycle.

✳ Lag your cylinder and pipes

Lagging the hot water cylinder will help reduce heat loss and thus cut your bills.

✳ Watch out for the big freeze

Check outside taps if cold weather is on the way – they are very vulnerable to freezing up. Shut off the supply from the service valve inside the house, and leave the outside tap turned on so that any residual water can expand when it freezes – that way you'll avoid burst pipes. If you see icicles forming on overflow pipes it is a sure sign that you have a leaky ball valve. Fix it before the ice blocks the overflow and floods the house.

Waste water and sewage

In most homes, the waste water from sinks and baths now flows into the main soil pipe, into which the toilet is also emptied. Older houses have external soil pipes, about 100mm (4in) across, running up the wall near to the bathroom. In modern houses, soil pipes commonly run inside the property, and are normally boxed in so they are not visible. At the top of the soil pipe there is usually a vent, normally above roof level, (but if not, it's because an air admittance valve is used instead). At the point where a waste pipe goes below ground it becomes a drain, which runs through an inspection chamber covered by a manhole – invaluable if there are problems or blockages – and from here it runs into the public sewer. The water collected in your gutters flows down the downpipe into either a soakaway (where it soaks into the ground) or into the public drain.

✳ Address hard water

If you live in a hard water area, this can have a detrimental effect on your appliances and your pipes over time. There are many options, the most effective of which is to install a water softener on the rising main above the cold water tap in the kitchen, which means that the water going everywhere else in the home is treated, but your drinking water is unaffected.

✳ Keep gutters and waste pipes clear

Scoop out leaves and debris from gutters once a year to prevent them from overflowing, but make sure the waste doesn't go down the downpipe. Ideally, cover the downpipe with mesh to prevent leaves being swept down. Remove ice in severe weather to reduce the weight in the gutters. In the kitchen, don't allow bits of food, oil and fat to go down the plughole as they can cause blockages.

Heating

There are numerous ways to heat homes and supply domestic hot water, most of which are based on some sort of boiler burning gas or oil, driving a water-based central heating system. This is not the only way, though. Increasingly, alternative systems such as underfloor and biomass heating are being used, and heat pumps are becoming an attractive alternative to boilers.

Central heating

Central heating heats your home from one main source - a boiler. Using gas or oil, the boiler heats water, which is then pumped to radiators and a hot water cylinder (if you have a conventional boiler).

The system is operated by a set of controls which usually include a clock or programmer, room thermostat and thermostatic radiator valves. These make sure the heating and hot water come on at a suitable time and temperature. I've programmed my heating to come on later at the weekend so it doesn't disturb my lie-in. Some programmes can split the top floor and the ground floor heating times, so you're not heating bedrooms when you're not in them.

If you're thinking of updating your boiler, here's a brief outline of the typical types. Do your research and check out a variety of companies to see what's best for you and your home. If space is an issue you can get boilers that fit in the roof (operated by remote control) or even ones that go outside.

A conventional boiler

This system has two water tanks in the loft – a large cold water storage tank (which refills from the cold water mains) and a small feed and expansion tank.

Water from the storage tank feeds cold water down to the cylinder (usually in the airing cupboard). The boiler heats the cylinder, converting cold water to hot. This hot water is then released to all the hot water taps in the house. A pump circulates the hot water through the pipes to heat the radiators.

A combi boiler

These are economical to run and give you a continuous supply of hot water – so you'll never run out of hot water in a deep bath. The flow may be limited if other taps are running at the same time (so not much fun when your partner turns the hose on in the garden when you're having a shower).

As the combi boiler heats water instantly, direct from the mains, there is no need to wait for a storage cylinder to heat up, and you won't run out of hot water. There's also no need for cold water storage tanks so you can fill your loft with lots more boxes! A pump circulates the hot water through the pipes and to heat the radiators.

What is a condensing boiler?

Condensing boilers use heat from exhaust gases that would normally be released into the atmosphere through the flue. Due to this process, it is able to extract more heat from the fuel it uses than a standard boiler. It also means that less heat is lost through the flue gases. The efficiency of a typical non-condensing boiler is around 75%, whereas with condensing boilers it can be over 87%.

Electric heating

Electric heating, in the form of night storage heaters, has been with us for many years. Although the heaters are quite bulky, the main objection of comparatively high running costs is no longer as significant as it once was with spiralling fossil fuel prices. The drawback of very slow response to temperature settings remains, however – it can take a day or more for thermostat changes to take effect.

Underfloor electric heating is another option, and this is an especially popular choice for bathrooms and kitchens. It is suitable for both new-build and retrospective installation, and leaves the walls clutter-free. Like storage heating, it is slow to respond to temperature changes, so you may need supplementary heating in sudden cold snaps.

www.theunderfloorheatingstore.com

Alternative heating

LPG

LPG (Liquefied Petroleum Gas) is the closest alternative to mains gas and is used for central heating, hot water and cooking. It can be stored in cylinders or in a tank (above or below ground).

Wood burning / Biomass

A biomass boiler is fuelled by solid wood pellets, chips or logs. These can fuel central heating radiators and water heating systems.

Warm Air Systems

Warm air systems supply heat into the rooms through vents in either the ceiling or walls. A warm air unit burns gas and the heat from this process is mixed with air and circulated around the property via a series of ducts in the ceiling and roof space.

Solar Thermal

Solar thermal panels capture rays of sunlight in order to heat water. They fix to your roof and use a heat transfer system to pass heat from the sun directly into the water in your cylinder. They can provide around 50% to 70% of a typical home's hot water because they don't rely on direct sunlight to work –just as well in the UK!

They use a special type of hot water tank so it's best to consider solar thermal panels when you are planning to replace your central heating system.

Avoid problems

✳ **Bleed radiators once a year**

It is inevitable that some air will get into the system, and this will cause the top of one radiator to become cooler – almost always the highest one. Left unbled, the problem can worsen and affect more radiators and it also provides a corrosive environment inside the radiators.

✳ **Watch out for corrosion**

If you have to bleed your heating system frequently, it may indicate that corrosion is taking place within the system. Get this checked and remedied before it gets bad enough to cause leaks or other problems.

Cold areas lower down on radiators indicate a build up of sludge in the system. You will need to drain and flush the system to clear this, and this can often mean removing the radiators to flush them effectively – it may be better to get this done professionally.

Any time the heating system is drained, even partially, make sure you top up using water with an inhibitor added. Plain water can accelerate corrosion problems in the system.

✳ **Service your central heating system regularly**

If you have gas central heating, use a Gas Safe registered engineer who is experienced with your make of boiler. Oil-fired systems should be serviced by an Oftec registered engineer who will be able to measure and document boiler efficiency as part of the procedure. Once a year is sensible, but try to get it done in spring or summer, before the rush when everybody turns their systems on in late autumn and finds they don't work. Older models will eventually get to the point where they are uneconomic to maintain, but at least it's an opportunity to upgrade to a more efficient and eco-friendly newer model.

✳ **Condensing boiler failure in cold weather**

It is possible for condensing boilers to fail in exceptionally cold weather. This can be caused by water freezing in the condensate pipe and blocking it. Try defrosting the pipe with some hot water. If this fixes the problem, you should insulate the external pipework to reduce the risk of another blockage.

✳ **Funny noises**

If you hear odd knocking or banging noises coming from your boiler (or from the hot water cylinder when the immersion heater is on) it may be 'kettling' – the noise your kettle sometimes makes just before it boils. You should check this out – it may indicate a buildup of limescale in the system, especially in hard water areas. Left unfixed, you could be in for major boiler or cylinder problems later.

Greener home

There are many things that you can do to make your home more environmentally friendly – and the great thing is that they will also save you money. Here are a few examples to get you started and also some considerations for the future.

Easy green options

✳ Cleaning
Toxic cleaning products are extremely harmful to the environment and are easily avoided by buying responsibly and hence stopping these chemicals from entering the water cycle.

✳ Fit a water butt
This is a straightforward job which involves finding a discreetly placed downpipe from your gutter (or non-discreet if you don't mind the sight of a water butt in your front garden!). You simply fit a diverter kit to the downpipe by cutting into it, fitting the sleeve and then attaching the hose to the butt. The water butt will then collect rainwater that flows down from your gutter and you can use it to water the garden, thus reducing your water consumption.

✳ Flushing
Fit a low-flush toilet, which will use considerably less water per flush than a standard cistern. There is an even quicker and cheaper way to do this by placing a heavy, non rusting object into your cistern (for example an old plastic bottle filled with sand) which will mean that the cistern doesn't require as much water to fill each time.

✳ Insulate your house
Later in the manual, we discuss insulation (loft, walls, pipes, hot water cylinder) and draught proofing, which are great ways to reduce your energy needs. There are also greener ways of insulating, using wool and newspaper-derived materials – worth investigating.

✳ Turn off lights
Turn off lights in rooms that aren't being used, and turn off and unplug appliances that aren't being used. If an appliance has a standby light, it's using electricity.

✳ Gardening
If you like gardening, then growing your own fruit and vegetables is a great pastime; it can save you money and ensure you're eating really well. It's also a great way to get some exercise.

✳ Compost
You can even make your own compost by putting your kitchen and garden waste to good use in a compost heap.

✳ Central Heating
Turning your central heating down a degree will hardly be noticeable to you, but will save you a significant amount on your heating bills. If you have thermostatic valves on individual radiators, then adjust them for each room, so that you're not heating a virtually unused guest bedroom to the same temperature as your living room, for example.

Recycling

Rather than contributing to landfill, take a few minutes each day to sort your rubbish into items that can be recycled and those that can't. Most homes in the UK now have a council organised collection service for materials which can be recycled – so think twice next time you go to throw your tins, glass, plastic, paper or cardboard in your normal bin.

✳ Plastics – Most plastics are by-products of petroleum, which is considered one of the largest contributors to global warming. Plastics frequently end up in landfill, so reducing your usage has a double impact. Reuse old shopping bags, or buy some hessian reusable bags instead and recycle anything you do use. On-line retailers are increasingly offering minimal-packaging versions of many products. Take advantage – less hassle for you, better for the planet, and possibly a bit cheaper.

✳ Paper – reduce the amount of paper that you use by taking a few simple steps. Sign up to a mail preference service (which is free) to reduce the amount of junk mail you receive. Not only does this help the environment but it saves you time and hassle too, and your postie will be most grateful. Also, you can take action such as opting for paper-free bank statements, bills online from service providers and so on.

Greener energy

Technology has progressed fast in this field in the last ten years and there are some amazing products available that can reduce or eliminate your reliance on the national grid for electricity. Solar energy works even in less sunny climates, and can meet a proportion of your energy needs. Check out the government's Feed-In Tariff scheme to see if installing a PVA (photovoltaic array) on your roof would be a money-saving and green option for you. You could even see a profit from the energy fed back into the grid. Domestic size wind turbines are now available, but do check with your planning department before having one installed as they are not small and you will most likely need permission. With these options, take care to chose a reputable installer, and be wary of the cowboys...

✳ Greener heat

Consider a green alternative, especially if your old boiler is on its last legs. Replacing it with a condensing boiler could save you money and lower your emissions. Switching to another fuel can be very expensive, but may be worth considering if you can accept a long payback period. Wood and derivative fuels are great because they are carbon-neutral (wood releases about the same amount of carbon as it absorbs while growing) so wood stoves and pellet stoves and boilers are worth considering, but only if you have a local supply of fuel and suitable storage facilities. Wood stoves are simpler and cheaper to install, but are mostly best regarded as room heater, perhaps with a back boiler to supplement water heating.

✳ Heat pumps

Heat pumps work rather like refrigerators or air conditioning in reverse. By cooling the environment outside the home, they harvest energy which can be used to heat the home. Ground source heat pumps work by using the heat from the ground to warm water and provide heating for your home, and can also work in reverse to provide cooling in the warmer months. They are expensive and disruptive to install, however, so are best suited to new-build homes. Air source heat pumps are cheaper and easier to install but are much less efficient, especially during winter when you need the heat most. Heat pumps are a promising new technology, but be wary of some wildly optimistic efficiency claims.

Kerrie's top tip

As information is constantly changing, go to www.energysavingtrust.org.uk to get the latest on heating, insulation and all other ways to save energy.

Greener shopping

Many of the things we buy regularly (and not so regularly) are far from green. With a little thought, it is possible to find better and more ethical alternatives to many of them. You don't need to get obsessive, but each time you choose the green option, you are helping a little.

FAIRTRADE

✳ In the supermarket, look out for Fairtrade products. These are good news for the producers, and are generally better environmentally than the mainstream equivalents.

✳ If you are shopping for timber products, look for the FSC (Forest Stewardship Council) logo to guarantee ethically-sourced timber.

✳ Instead of installing a hardwood floor, consider using bamboo. It is environmentally friendly material as it grows very quickly and therefore replenishes itself in just 4–6 years, as opposed to 50–100 years for hardwoods.

✳ Buying a new gadget? Check out the manufacturer's website to find out their policy on their carbon footprint, emissions, packaging reduction and recycling policy.

✳ Buy appliances with low energy ratings (washing machines, fridges etc), and buy energy saving light bulbs for all your fittings.

✳ Stop buying disposable batteries and switch to rechargeables instead.

Try to use rechargeable batteries

DECORATING

Decorating is often the only thing that a novice DIYer will attempt. It is an incredibly rewarding job to tackle as the results are really clear to see and can transform the look and feel of a room, without enormous amounts of effort. There are many options to choose from, from plain painted walls, to paint effects, or the use of wallpaper as a feature wall or for the whole room. Whatever you choose the basics will be explained in this chapter. Once you've gained confidence, why not try creating something a little more unique, such as alternating several bands of differing shades of the same colour around the room. With a spirit level and some masking tape, and a little imagination, you can achieve something very special.

Good preparation is the most important part of the job

Painting

Decorating is probably the most underestimated professional trade there is. It looks easy, so it's one of the most likely things for enthusiastic but clueless DIYers to have a go at. Sometimes, sadly, with catastrophic results.

While it's not rocket science there are a few basic things you need to know to achieve a really good and long-lasting finish. The key is in the preparation, a stage often completely overlooked by DIYers – but this is where us women have a major advantage with our natural attention to detail. It's not glamorous, and it's not as exciting as painting that gorgeous new colour, but it makes all the difference between an OK finish and a great one.

Stencils can be very effective on painted walls

Test out colours in daylight and artificial light as there can be a dramatic difference

The right type

There are two main types of paint – oil-based and water-based. The clue is on the tin where it describes how to wash the brushes afterwards – if it involves white spirit it's oil-based paint; if you only need soapy water, it's water-based.

Both have their merits, although oil-based paint may not be on the shelves much longer. It's already been banned in America for its environmental impact if incorrectly disposed of down the drains.

Water-Based Paint

This is often called emulsion, and is most commonly used for walls and ceilings, and covering large areas using a combination of brush and roller. It is easy to apply, it's relatively easy to clean drips or spots off clothes or carpets if you spill it (try not to let it dry), and much cheaper per litre than other paints.

Water-based paint comes in a variety of tin sizes from 1, 2.5 and 5 litres right up to 10 and sometimes 15 litres. If you are working on your own I would suggest buying 5-litre tins at the largest, as the big ones can be very heavy and difficult to handle – not just when you buy them, but also when you try and decant the paint into trays and paint kettles.

Masonry paint is also a water-based paint specifically designed for use outside. Never use regular emulsion outside as it won't last. Masonry paint normally has crushed sand or crushed stones in it to fill small cracks and make it durable enough to resist weather, frost, sunlight and so on.

Oil-Based Paint

This is also now referred to as solvent-based paint as in reality oil isn't always used. This paint is designed for use on woodwork (internal and external) and metalwork. It comes in gloss and satin/eggshell finishes. Gloss shows up more imperfections, so thorough preparation is essential. Oil-based paint is trickier to use than water-based paint as it takes longer to dry (6–24 hours) and can run and drip, especially around mouldings and features. The woodwork section later in this chapter will show you how to avoid this happening. This type of paint is much more hard-wearing and durable than water-based paint, so is ideal for protecting exterior and interior woodwork. Brushes will need to be cleaned in white spirit or a similar solution, and neither the paint nor the white spirit should be disposed of down a sink, toilet or drain as the chemicals are harmful to fish and the environment. Your local tip should have a recycling facility for all paints and solutions.

Characteristic	Water-Based	Oil-Based	Comments
Ease Of Application	✳ ✳ ✳ ✳ ✳	✳ ✳ ✳	Water-based tend to be much easier to apply, with less 'brushing out' required
Drying Time	✳ ✳ ✳ ✳ ✳	✳	Much quicker turn-around between coats with water-based paints
Low Odour/Taint	✳ ✳ ✳ ✳ ✳	✳	White-spirit smell of solvent-based paints can be overpowering. Minimal problem with water-based
Washability	✳ ✳ ✳	✳ ✳ ✳ ✳ ✳	Surfaces painted with solvent-based paints are easiest to clean
Durability	✳ ✳ ✳	✳ ✳ ✳ ✳ ✳	Solvent-based are more hard-wearing, although water-based are catching up with improved formulation
Brushmarks	✳ ✳	✳ ✳ ✳ ✳	More evident in water-based, although improving all the time
Colour Retention	✳ ✳ ✳ ✳	✳ ✳ ✳	White solvent-based (especially) tends to yellow with age
Cleaning Tools	✳ ✳ ✳ ✳ ✳	✳	Water-based easily cleaned with water and mild detergent. Solvent-based is a lengthier process requiring white spirit
User-Friendly	✳ ✳ ✳ ✳	✳	All health and safety guidelines make water-based products a better option than their solvent-based counterparts

Paint finishes

It is really important, if you want to achieve a great finish, to use the right type of paint for the job. The table below lays out the main types of paint that are available to the DIYer, and what makes them different to each other, as well as showing you where they are best used. Equally important is to build up the layers in the correct order, for example starting with primers on bare surfaces, followed by undercoat and topcoat. Some are more difficult than others to apply, but don't be put off by this as practice makes perfect. You will live to regret it if you try and take a short cut and use the wrong paint as the finish won't look great and the paint won't last and will start to peel or flake and you'll end up with more work than when you started.

How much emulsion?

* Tins will specify the average coverage, but it's normally around 11 square metres per litre.
* For the walls of a room 4m x 4m, allowing two coats, buy 5 litres.
* If you are having paint mixed to a specific colour, buy slightly more than you think you'll need.
* If you do run out of a custom mix there are some cheats, such as painting one complete wall in the new batch, which lessens the effect of the difference due to the different light angle.

Kerrie's top tip

Beware of false economy in buying paint, especially water-based paint. Cheaper paints often have a much lower opacity, which means they are much thinner, and you can end up having to apply five or six coats.

Type	Product Description	Suitable Surfaces	Main Qualities	Limitations	Application Method
Primer	Watery, dilute appearance specifically formulated to seal bare surfaces	All bare wood, plaster or metal. Specific or all-purpose primers are available	Excellent sealer enabling application of further coats of paint	Only use on bare surfaces	Brush. May use roller or spray with water-based primers
Primer-Undercoat	A primer and undercoat in one, providing base for top coat(s)	Bare wood	Easy to use, and time-saving	Not as hard-wearing as oil-based undercoat	Brush, roller or spray
Undercoat	Dull, opaque finish providing ideal base for application of top coat(s)	Any primed surface	Hard-wearing	Application takes longer than primer-undercoat	Brush or roller
Matt Emulsion	All purpose matt-finish paint. Water–based	Plaster surfaces	A thinned first coat acts as an excellent primer. Apply full strength coats to finish	Not hard-wearing	Brush, roller or spray
Vinyl Emulsion	Available in a number of finishes from matt to silk. Water-based	On primed or previously painted plaster surfaces, or direct to lining paper	Vinyl qualities make it easy to clean	When 'cutting in' with dark colours, framing effect difficult to avoid	Brush, roller or spray
Eggshell	Mid-sheen finishing paint. Proprietary variations on this theme	Any primed or undercoated surface	More hard-wearing than emulsions	Slight sheen tends to accentuate imperfections on large surface areas	Brush or roller; spray with water-based
Gloss	Shiny 'polished' finishing paint	Any undercoated surface, ideally wood or metal	Very hard-wearing decorative finish. Easy to clean	Application is time consuming and requires a sound technique	Brush or roller
Textured Paint	Textured relief paint, that can be used as a finish or overpainted	Plaster surfaces	Adds further decorative dimension to flat walls or ceilings. Excellent for hiding rough surfaces	Difficult to clean. Difficult to remove if redecoration required	Roller, brush, combs/variety of finishing tools

Caring for tools

Caring for tools. Knowledge, practice and skill will get you a long way in achieving a great finish, but berating the saying "a bad workman blames his tools" is a little misguided. If your brushes are trashed, your rollers knackered and your paint tin full of lumps of dried paint, your walls are not going to look nice. Therefore caring for your tools and your paint is crucial, and here are some tips.

* To keep your paint fresh always make sure the lip around the top of the tin, and the lid are free from paint, so that the lid closes fully and tightly. Wherever possible decant your paint into a tray or paint kettle when working, to avoid dipping back into the tin and transferring dust, lumps and bumps from the brush into the tin. Keep your paint in a cool place, but not too cold where there's a risk of freezing.

* To keep your brushes in top condition wash them really thoroughly at the end of each day, using the appropriate cleaner for the paint you're using, ie washing up liquid and hot water for water-based paints, and white spirit for oil-based paints. When using white spirit, be careful it doesn't go down the drain as it's harmful to the environment. Wash the brushes in a jam jar of white spirit and then give them a final wash with washing up liquid and hot water.

* Store brushes lying flat so that bristles don't get damaged. There are some storage boxes for oil brushes on the market that have a vapour bottle in them that prevent the brushes from drying out. These are great but don't be tempted just to stick the brushes straight in before cleaning them, as over time the paint will build up and ruin the brushes.

* Roller trays should be washed out to remove all wet paint. Some emulsion can dry on and won't harm subsequent use, but don't leave large quantities in the tray. If it gets really thick you may actually be able to peel it off in large chunks, but this is time consuming and grubby work, so it's best just to clean as you go.

* Rollers are probably most people's least favourite thing to clean. You can get away with wrapping them up tightly in a plastic bag or cling film overnight if you're going to paint again the next day, but any longer and they'll dry out. Once you're finished, wash them under running hot water and add a tiny amount of washing up liquid. More than a drop or two will have you rinsing out bubbles for hours. Hold the roller upright under the tap and gradually stroke the paint out from top to bottom, turning it each time and working around the roller until the water starts to run more clear. You will never get to the point of it being completely clear unless you have the patience of a saint, and in my experience you don't need to as getting the majority of the paint out is sufficient.

Look after your tools and they will last for years

Painting tools

It may be slightly sad, but buying decorating bits and pieces is my idea of a good shopping trip – I'm not interested in clothes shopping, but put me in the decorating aisle of a DIY shop and I'm in my element! That said, I've tried to contain my excitement and just lay out the basics you will need to get started, but if you're anything like me, you'll be adding to your collection every time you buy more paint.

Preparation

Sandpaper and block
Buy a pack of sandpaper containing different grades of roughness as they can be used for different tasks, such as rubbing down rough filler or creating a 'key' (slightly roughened surface) ready for oil-based paint. A block will help in larger areas as you can wrap the sandpaper around it and be a little rougher and faster.

Masking tape
Prevents paint getting on windows, carpet, glass, etc.

Sugar soap
Cleans walls prior to painting.

Filling knife and scraper
The key to a good filling knife is flexibility; make sure there is some bend in the blade as this will help you achieve a good result. On the flip side, a scraper should be stiff as this is used for heavier duty tasks such as wallpaper stripping.

Shave hook
A shave hook is just a triangular-shaped scraper designed to get into hard-to-reach corners and decorative mouldings.

Dust sheets
To protect floors and furniture.

Fillers

All-purpose filler
For holes and cracks.

Ready-mixed filler
For holes and cracks.

Stainable filler
For wood that will have a see-through finish, eg stain.

Knotter
Seals bleeding knots in wood.

Flexible filler (caulk)
For joints and cracks where movement is likely.

Painting

Ladder and ladder hooks

You will need a stepladder for 'cutting in' (doing the fiddly bits round the edges – see later) the walls and ceiling, and reaching high woodwork such as picture rails or the tops of windows. Make sure it's sturdy, but light and easy to carry around. Also buy a ladder hook, which is a metal hook you can attach your paint kettle to as this will leave one hand free to hold on, and one hand free to paint. Don't balance a kettle, tin or tray on the top step, unless it's a proper platform – it will end in tears. If you are planning on exterior decorating you will need a ladder and/or scaffold boards. Unless you have a huge amount to do, it's probably best to hire these as they can be expensive and difficult to store, given their size. You can also hire ladder stand-offs to attach to the top of the ladder, which will give you access to overhanging areas such as facias and soffits.

Brushes

A set of four different size brushes is a good start – 12mm, 25mm, 50mm and 100mm. The 12mm will be useful for intricate oil-based work, the 25mm and 50mm for normal oil-based work, and 100mm is perfect for water-based paint.

Fitches

For detailed work.

Lid opener

A flat headed screwdriver will also do this job.

Rollers and trays

These are essential to make walls and ceilings quick and easy to paint. I would recommend starting with two trays and two rollers so that you can have two colours on the go at once (maybe white for the ceiling and a colour on the walls) without having to wash them up each time. Rollers and trays can be wrapped up tightly in plastic bags overnight to prevent them drying out, which can save a lot of washing and gallons of water. Foam rollers are cheapest but they tend to spatter you and everything else, so go for mohair or lambs wool. If the surfaces are smooth short pile or medium pile are best – but you will need long pile for rough or textured surfaces (such as an artexed ceiling or masonry paint for outside walls).

Paint kettle

A lot of DIYers don't bother to get a paint kettle (essentially just an empty pot, made of plastic or metal, with a handle) but I highly recommend you buy one or two as they are much easier to handle than carrying the whole paint tub around – plus if there is an accident, you have a smaller quantity of paint to deal with! They are also easier to take up and down ladders and hang off ladder hooks.

Preparation

The importance of preparation cannot be overstated. There is nothing more frustrating than having to repaint something because of bad planning. If you want to get a truly professional finish, then this is the area to spend plenty of time and invest serious elbow grease in.

* Start by clearing the space you are going to be working in as much as possible.
* Remove all pictures from walls, clear all shelves and fireplaces, remove lamp shades and take into a different room as much furniture as possible.
* Larger pieces that cannot be removed should be moved to the middle of the room (ideally not under a light fitting as you'll need to get to this with your step ladder to cut in).
* Cover anything that is left (including floors) with dust sheets or protective sheeting.
* Take down curtains and remove curtain poles, remove handles from doors (but keep a large flat head screwdriver which fits the handle hole in case the door closes with no handles!).

Preparation should follow a particular order. However, you can jump around a little to suit your schedule, for example if you're waiting for some filler to dry before you can sand it, move onto something else. Ideally work downwards – start with the ceiling, then the walls, then the woodwork.

Hiding stains

If you have any damp patches or marks then they need to be dealt with, otherwise they will bleed through the paint. Any mould or surface marks should have washed off at the sugar soaping stage. You will then need to cover the stain with a stain block. There are some great products on the market depending on the severity of the stain. Some come in spray cans and are very easy to apply – these tend to be best for small, lighter-coloured stains. The more industrial-strength products tend to come in tins and need to be painted on. Read the instructions thoroughly as they often take up to 24 hours to dry. Sometimes more than one layer will be needed – you will know this if you can still see the stain when the blocker is dry. Don't be tempted to use the same brush for other paints as it can cross infect other products.

Ceilings and walls

1 Start by washing them down with diluted sugar soap (don't forget protective eye wear) and then rinse and allow to dry. This will remove any dirt or old adhesive and leave a sound base for painting. Make sure you don't get water on light switches or plug sockets.

2 If there are small cracks in corners then you'll need the correct filler, which is called caulk. The easiest way to apply this is with a caulk gun directly into the crack. Don't apply too much as it will stand out and look too obvious.

3 Then run a clean finger (or a smooth cloth) over the line of caulk to smooth it. Areas that need caulking are usually corners of walls, points where walls meet cornices or skirtings, and around door frames. It's amazing what a difference having these gaps filled will make to the final appearance.

Filler masterclass

If there are cracks and holes away from corners then you will need to use filler and your filling knife. It's easiest to use a ready mixed filler (I favour one that is very light and has a marshmallow type consistency as it's very easy to get smooth and can fill large holes in one visit).

1 Make sure the area to be filled is sound by using your scraper to remove any loose plaster, if necessary enlarging the crack or hole. Remove any dust with an old paint brush.

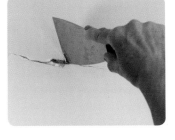

2 Apply filler with your filling knife at right angles to the crack as this will ensure it gets right in and leaves it level with the edge of the crack.

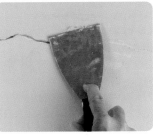

3 Remove any excess filler by turning your filling knife around and drawing it along the crack.

* It is hard to get this right first time and it really doesn't matter – just keep adding more filler if necessary and removing excess over and over again until it's full and reasonably flat.

* When it's dry, give the area a light sand with sandpaper to ensure a smooth finish that won't show up once it's painted.

* It is a good idea to give the whole surface a light sand to remove any little splodges, lumps and bumps, affectionately called 'bogies' in the trade! Stubborn bogies may need helping on their way with your scraper.

Woodwork

Wooden window frames and sills, skirting boards, dado rails and picture rails, as well as door frames and doors, also need thorough preparation. Make sure you do this before you start painting the walls as otherwise you will damage your paintwork and need to start at the beginning again.

1 If the wood is bare and new, it will need a solution called 'knotting' applied over any knots in the wood. This is easily painted on and will prevent sap from bleeding through the paintwork.

* If sap is bleeding through existing paintwork, rub it down with sandpaper until the area around the knot is bare, and apply knotting solution.

* Caulk and filler can be applied to any cracks and holes as described earlier, but this time use specialist wood filler as it dries harder and doesn't contain water, which could rot or swell the wood.

2 Once all the fillers and knotting solution are dry, all wooden surfaces need to be rubbed down to a smooth finish. Try and go with the grain of the wood where possible.

* It's best to avoid stripping paint if at all possible. Paint from before around 1960 may contain lead and can be very hazardous, so always wear a protective mask whether stripping it or sanding it.

3 Finally, wipe down the woodwork with some white spirit and ensure any dust is removed.

4 Paint primer on to any bare areas of wood to seal it and prepare the surface for undercoat and top coat.

Cutting in

All ceilings and walls will need to be 'cut in' before you can begin rolling on the paint. Cutting in means applying paint to the edges and corners, by brush, so that the main sections left to paint are large, flat, obstacle-free areas suitable for rolling.

Remember – don't overload your brush

It is important to cut in a ceiling or wall before you begin using the roller so that you can eliminate unsightly brush marks and obtain a more professional result.

You can use a large or small emulsion brush for this task – whatever you feel more comfortable with. A small brush should be held like a pen, while a large brush should be held like a table tennis bat. Try and hold the brush bristles perpendicular to the line as you are cutting in, you will obtain a much neater result and a straighter line.

It is a good idea to use a paint kettle rather than working directly from the paint pot. Kettles are easier to handle, and you can hang them from a hook on your stepladder. When loading

paint onto the brush, don't be shy – give the brush a good dunk, but stop before the paint reaches the metal part of the brush that holds the bristles. Then, to avoid drips, remove excess paint by gently brushing the bristles against the edge of the kettle.

1 Place your stepladder in one corner of the room, and make sure you have your paint kettle securely attached to it. Then climb up it, load the brush as above, hold the brush with bristles upright and tuck them into the corner between the wall and the ceiling. This will help guide your brush in a straight line. If you have coving, use the bottom of this as your guide. Cut in as far along the top of both walls as you can reach comfortably without stretching too far, and make sure you paint down around 10cm from the ceiling all the way around.

2 Before moving your ladder, also cut in the corner of the wall down to a height that you will be able to reach from the floor without a ladder – this will save you having to go round again with the ladder to paint the corners.

3 Continue around the room, cutting in the top of the wall and the top section of the corners of the wall. When you reach another obstacle such as a window, or a picture rail, cut in the parts of these which can only be reached by ladder – again this will save you time and ensure that everything else can be reached from the floor.

4 Once you have gone all the way around the room fold the ladder out of the way and begin the bottom sections, joining the cutting in of the top corners you've already done down to skirting level, and continuing along the top of the skirting boards.

5 Cut in the bottom half of windows and any other areas you couldn't reach from the step-ladder, and in particular look out for plug sockets and light switches.

Walls & ceilings

The hardest bit is now over and the fun bit can begin when you actually start to see an improvement, rather than deterioration, in the appearance of your room. There is a set order in which to paint a room – follow it, otherwise you'll be making work for yourself. Start with the ceiling, followed by walls, windows, doors and frames, picture and dado rails and finally the skirting boards.

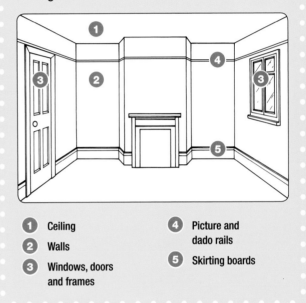

1 Ceiling

2 Walls

3 Windows, doors and frames

4 Picture and dado rails

5 Skirting boards

6 Cutting in a ceiling is exactly the same process as cutting in a wall with the exception that you will need to work from a stepladder all the time, and if you are painting the walls afterwards you don't have to be quite so careful about neat edges, as you will be cutting in over them with your wall colour later. Start in the corner and work your way around the room, ensuring you cut in to the ceiling around 10cm, then cut around any light fittings.

If you have decorative coving you will need to paint this by hand too before you begin rolling, so do this at the same time as you cut in the main part of the ceiling.

Now you are ready to fill in the areas between your cutting in, using a roller or a paint pad.

Rolling

Using a roller is the quickest and most efficient way of covering large surface areas. Rollers can be used to apply solvent-based paints, but they are most often used with water-based paints such as emulsion or acrylic eggshell.

Extension pole
– for hard to
reach areas

A roller tray consists of two parts: the paint reservoir, and a ribbed slope to wipe off excess paint and allow it to run back into the reservoir. Pour the prepared paint into the tray's reservoir, filling it to just below the start of the slope.

Kerrie's top tip

When you have to pause during painting, between coats for example, wrap a length of cling film around the roller head. This saves having to wash out and dry the roller at frequent intervals.

Dip the roller head into the paint reservoir and run it firmly up and down the ribs of the slope to distribute the paint evenly round the roller. Take care not to overload the head or paint will drip and splatter everywhere.

1 Starting with the ceiling, either using an extension pole, or working from a stepladder, work in blocks of around a metre, starting near the window.

Work quickly so that the edge of your previous block is still wet when you join it up with the next block; this will avoid creating marks.

2 To get the best possible coverage roll first in one direction and then over the same area in the opposite direction across the previous roller marks – this will also help avoid leaving marks where the edge of the roller was.

Don't overload the roller with paint as half of it will spatter down onto you and the dustsheets, and marks are more likely. You may well find, especially if the ceiling hasn't been painted for a few years, that two or more coats are necessary, in which case do exactly the same with the second coat, starting with cutting in, then rolling away from the window.

How many coats?

* Most walls will need at least two coats of paint
* You may be extremely lucky and get away with one coat if the colour is very similar to what's underneath, and if the paint's very good quality.
* Deeper colours and drastic colour changes will require three or more coats.
* Before packing away your rollers after the last coat, wait until the paint is fully dry to see how good the finish is; you can't get an accurate idea while it's still wet.

3 Painting the walls is very similar to the ceiling, although it's easier to move around. Again you may prefer to use an extension pole rather than a stepladder to reach the top third of the wall – whatever you are most comfortable with. If you are right-handed, start your first block in the top right-hand corner of the window wall (reverse this if you are left-handed).

4 I like working down the wall, then starting at the top next to my original block, but it's just as effective to work across the wall then come back to the right-hand side for the next block down. Again, work quickly to ensure that the edges of your previous blocks are still wet when you paint the next block. The same technique applies of rolling in one direction and then immediately rolling across those lines in the opposite direction, to ensure good coverage and minimal roller marks.

5 You can get special small, thin radiator rollers to paint the area of wall behind a radiator, and these can also be useful for smaller areas of wall such as above doors, above windows, and the inside of a window reveal. They can be better than using a brush in these areas as the dappled finish will then match the rest of the rolled wall.

Small and thin radiator roller

Using paint pads

Paint pads make less spray and mess than rollers. Their design has been improved in recent years, so now they can be used successfully, not just for covering large flat surfaces, but also for small, intricate areas such as window beads, door architraves and for cutting in.

1 Paint pads are flat and rectangular with closely packed, short, fine fibres. They produce a smooth paint finish when used carefully. Pads come in a range of sizes for all-round use.

2 When loading a paint pad, gently dip the fibres into the tray reservoir. Take care not to immerse the pad head, as this will cause drips when it is used on the wall. Pull the pad over the ribbed slope to distribute the paint evenly.

3 To paint the wall, use light even strokes in all directions, slightly overlapping each stroke. Pads need reloading more often than rollers as their fibres cannot hold as much paint. Paint pads tend to be faster than a brush but slower than a roller. There may be a need for extra coats as although pads apply paint very evenly, they tend to produce thinner coats. Extension poles can be attached to paint-pad heads to reach awkward areas such as ceilings.

Woodwork

Windows can be fiddly to paint, but by working in an organised way you can keep frustration to a minimum, and achieve a good result. Doing a thorough job on windows is particularly important: of all areas in the home, they are most affected by exterior climatic changes.

Choose a dry day to paint windows

A lot of people are scared about tackling woodwork as it is more complicated than walls and ceilings and also means using oil-based paint, which in itself is scary to start with. That said, once you get the hang of it, it may well become one of your favourite tasks, as the finishes you can achieve with oil-based paints are amazing compared to emulsion. As it tends to be the last thing you do in a room, it really is that stage where you see the incredible transformation become complete. So don't be scared, grab your brush and get started.

Masking areas

If you are not confident about getting neat edges you can mask off areas with masking tape, but make sure you don't remove this until the paint is completely dry.

Don't cut corners – cut some tape

Windows

These can be fiddly, but it's easier if you follow a specific order when painting both sash and casement windows, to achieve a better finish.

* One good tip – start early, so the paint will be dry enough to close the window at night.
* Ensure that your brush doesn't have too much paint on it as it's likely to pool in the corners and cause drips.
* It is, blissfully, no longer necessary to apply a separate undercoat and top coat as there are many combined products on the market. These also tend to be slightly thicker and therefore easier for the DIYer to handle.

Order of painting
Start by painting the areas that open ❶ ❷
Then paint the non-opening parts around the glass ❸
Finish by painting the outer frame and sill ❹

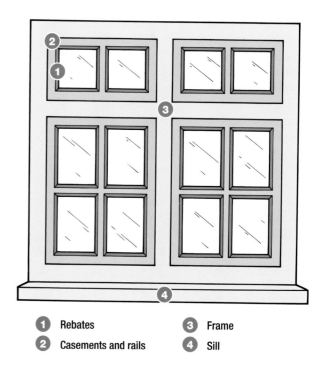

❶ Rebates   ❸ Frame
❷ Casements and rails   ❹ Sill

Sash windows

Due to their design, sash windows appear to be difficult to paint, but if the correct sequence of painting is followed, they are as straightforward as any other painting job.

If the runners are in sound, painted condition they are best left alone, as too many coats of paint will make the window jam.

1 Open the window slightly at both top and bottom, and start by painting the top half of the outer sash rebates. Move on to the horizontal and vertical rails.

2 Raise the inner sash until it is nearly at the top of the frame and pull down the outer sash. Finish off painting the rebates, horizontal and vertical rails on the outer sash. Then paint the inner sash rebates.

3 Leave the sashes in the same position as step 2, and finish painting the inner sash. Then paint the exposed lower runners, taking care not to touch or smudge the wet paint just applied to either of the sashes.

4 Return the window to its original position (step 1) and paint the upper runners. The top and bottom edges of the inner sash can now be painted. Finally, paint the surrounding frame and sill.

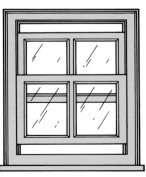

Painting radiators

* You don't need specialist radiator paint for radiators and pipes – you can use the same oil-based gloss or satin finish paint that you're using on the woodwork. Two coats of gloss paint are better than an undercoat and single gloss coat.

* Never paint a hot radiator – make sure it's turned off and cooled down before you start, and always allow the paint to dry fully before turning it back on.

* Start with all the fiddly bits like the top edge, side edges, pipes and so on.

* Then get to work on the main front area where the recesses go in and out. Make sure you overlap the top and bottom and work the paint right into the indents.

* You can be as messy as you like with your brush strokes as long as you finish them off in a neat top to bottom movement.

* Finally, work around the top and bottom faces (brush strokes from side to side) and the left and right faces (brush strokes top to bottom) rather like a panel door.

* Check for any areas of pooling paint or drips, and make sure you leave your dust sheet or some newspaper under all parts of the radiator for a few hours in case something drips off – this is very common, with all the nooks and crannies where paint can gather.

Flush doors

Flush doors are very easy to paint and I can help you with a big cheat here (don't tell the professionals).

1 Use a small sponge roller and little tray to apply the paint all over the door, quickly and evenly.

'Lay off' the paint with a medium brush

2 Then use a medium to large brush to 'lay off' the paint. This means drag the brush lightly over the surface in straight lines, working from the bottom to the top of the door and ensuring your brush overlaps the previous line each time as you move across the door.

✳ This will leave your door with an authentic 'brush applied' finish in about a quarter of the time it would have taken if you'd done the lot by brush.

✳ Wait until the paint is totally dry before replacing door handles and other fittings.

Panel doors

Panel doors are a little trickier, but (perhaps sadly) these are one of my favourite things to paint!

There is a set sequence to follow to get a great finish, as shown in this diagram and following step-by-steps.

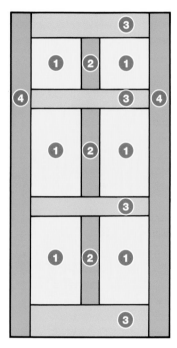

● Stiles

● Members

● Panels

1 Start with the internal returns (the sunken bits round the edges of the panels) and make sure your last strokes follow the grain of the wood. Then fill in the panels themselves, ensuring you leave your last brush marks going with the grain (top to bottom).

2 Fill in the vertical area between the panels with brush strokes from top to bottom.

3 Fill in the top, middle and bottom areas of the door with brush strokes from left to right.

4 Finally, paint the two side panels with brush strokes from top to bottom.

5 When you have completed this sequence, before leaving the door to dry, have a quick check of the corners to make sure paint hasn't pooled or started to drip. If it has, just spread it out with your brush in the same direction as the underlying brush strokes.

Other woodwork

Your room will really be starting to look great by this stage, so hang in there and keep on being careful so you don't spoil the finish. These items can be tricky to paint as they require a very steady hand for cutting in along edges that meet walls.

Use masking tape if you're not confident of getting a neat edge, but the underlying paint on the walls must be bone dry, otherwise when you take the tape off it will peel off the paint underneath.

You can buy low tack masking tape, which is handy for this job, but whatever you use, don't push it down too hard onto the walls, and take it off very gently and carefully as soon as you've painted the woodwork – even if it is still wet.

Colour divisions

If you have a different colour on your woodwork in adjoining rooms, then there is a set method to follow for where to finish one colour and where to start the next. Following this will ensure that one colour is visible from one direction, and the other colour from the other direction.

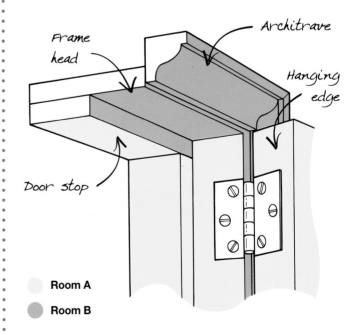

Frame head

Architrave

Hanging edge

Door stop

○ Room A
● Room B

Wallpapering

This is not the easiest job to tackle, but it's by no means impossible. If you haven't papered before I would suggest having a go at lining paper before tackling patterned paper, as it's more forgiving.

Lining

Flat undecorated paper hung on bare wall surfaces prior to hanging decorative wallpaper.

Standard Pattern

Flat wallpaper that has had a coloured design machine printed on to its surface.

Woodchip

Consists of two layers of paper bonded together with small chips of wood sealed between them. It provides a textured finish that is excellent for disguising rough wall surfaces. It should be painted after application.

Hand-printed

There are two main categories: screen printed or block printed. Both are printed one roll at a time. Pattern matching is often difficult and edges may need trimming before hanging. Usually expensive but the overall effect can be stunning.

Embossed

A relief pattern is imprinted in the paper during manufacture, producing a raised decorative surface. Some are white and are usually painted once hung, while others are already decorated. Take care not to flatten the relief during application.

Flock

Decorated with a pattern that has been cut into fibres built into the surface. Originally these were made from silk or wool, but today synthetic equivalents are more common and easier to hang. The pattern is mounted on flat backing paper.

Getting started

Wallpaper has increased in popularity again recently, particularly for feature walls – however, avoid thin paper, foils, flocks and fabrics if you are inexperienced as they are very difficult to work with and although they can look stunning, they will look downright awful if not applied properly. I'm going to talk you through papering a whole room, but the same techniques can be applied to a single wall or chimney breast.

Choosing the right paper

* If you are planning to paper an area that becomes steamy (no, not the bedroom) choose washable wallpaper.

* If your walls are very uneven, choose woodchip or embossed paper.

* Warm colours draw a surface towards you and can create a cosy effect.

* Cool colours take the surface away from you and creates an impression of space.

* Horizontal stripes trick the eye into thinking a small room is bigger than it actually is.

* Vertical stripes draw the eye upwards and therefore appear to heighten a room.

* Large patterns bring walls towards you and can be used to best effect in large rooms.

* Small patterns, like cool colours, create an illusion of space so work best in small rooms.

Quantity of rolls

There are all sorts of complicated mathematical equations you can get tied up with here, but the easy way is to cut a bit of wood or string to the width of your chosen wallpaper (normally 52cm) then work your way around the room with it to calculate how many full length drops you will need. Then measure skirting to ceiling, and add a margin of error of, say, 10cm to work out how long a full drop is. You can now work out how many drops you get per roll, and hence how many rolls to buy.

Here's an example: Your room requires 30 strips, and each roll provides 5 strips, so you need 6 rolls. If you are using patterned paper, buy extra as there is more wastage matching up the pattern.

It is crucial that the paper you buy is all from the same batch as otherwise colours and patterns can vary. Batch numbers are printed on the label.

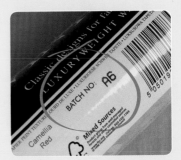

Buy extra paper when you need to match up the pattern

Plan the walls in a room and try mixing wallpaper with strong blocks of paint

Papering tools

Wallpapering is a reasonably specialist technique, and consequently requires some specialist equipment. The items you need aren't too expensive and worth investing in if you're planning to do a couple of rooms.

Straight edge (metre stick)
Ideally steel, for measuring out strips and using as a cutting edge.

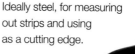

Bucket
To mix the paste and an old stick to stir it with, as well as a wide brush for pasting.

Folding pasting table
Don't be tempted to use your dining table as you might damage it, and it will actually make your papering much harder. You can buy pasting tables with centimetre markings on which are really useful. If not, you can put your own markings on, but make sure you use a pen that won't run when covered with wet paper.

Don't use your dining table!

Scissors
A sharp pair of scissors are a must for trimming the paper lengths to size before pasting and much easier to use than a knife.

Pencil
A pencil for marking out the cuts to make.

Clean cloth/Sponge
A clean cloth or sponge and a bucket of clean warm water for cleaning the table between pastings and also for wiping excess paste from the face of the paper when hanging.

Preparation

* Walls should be prepared as if for painting (see page 46) – holes and cracks filled, walls rubbed down and washed to remove dirt and dust.
* A bare plaster wall needs 'sizing' which means that you paint on a diluted solution of wallpaper paste and water (or using a specific sizing solution) all over the surface so that the wallpaper paste on the back of the paper will then dry evenly. It will also provide extra bite.

Measuring tape
A measuring tape is useful for measuring the wall to calculate the drop length you need.

Plumb line
A plumb line or chalk line is very handy to help you mark out a vertical line as a starting point; if not, a spirit level will do.

Trimming knife
This needs to be razor sharp as otherwise it can tear the edges of the paper.

Hanging brush
A hanging brush to help you smooth out the paper as you apply it.

Pasting brush
A wide brush for applying paste to the back of the wallpaper. It doesn't have to be a pasting brush though – a very wide, clean paint brush will do.

Wallpaper stripper
This gadget will help you strip off old paper much faster by generating steam which helps to release the old paper and its paste from the wall, making it easier to scrape off.

Stripping paper

If the walls have been previously papered, especially if the paper isn't stable, it should be stripped first, ideally using a steamer. When using a steam stripper, always read the instructions first.

1 Put on goggles and gloves and place the stripper's steam pad firmly on the wallpaper, holding it in place for about 30 seconds. Sometimes it may need a bit longer.

2 Move the pad across the wall and using a scaper, strip off the loose, bubbling paper. Take care not to dig the end of the scaper into the wall. You will soon build up a rhythm of stripping paper with one hand and steaming the next piece with the other.

If you don't have access to a steam stripper, you can buy stripping tablets which you add to a bucket of water. You then brush the solution onto sections of wallpaper and once it's soaked in, strip it away with a scaper.

The top layer of vinyl paper can often be pulled off easily – but make sure you still remove the backing paper as it won't be a suitable surface to decorate.

Paper-hanging

Make sure all old paper and adhesive is removed, and any nicks in the wall caused by scraping are filled. New plaster should be left a year before being papered, and should first be sealed. Then you are ready to set up your papering kit and tackle the room.

There are standard methods of laying out a room for papering. The general rule is to start just under one paper width to the side of the largest window, working towards the door. (The exception is if you are using a patterned paper and you have a chimney breast, in which case start with one length right in the middle of the chimney breast.

start in the middle of a chimney breast

1 Measure a couple of centimetres under a width, and pin the top of your chalk line to the top of the wall. Let the weight at the bottom come to rest, then hold it and ping the string of the line – this should leave a chalk line imprinted on the wall (because the string line itself is covered in chalk). Use this mark as a guide to line up your paper. If you are using a traditional plumb line, mark the line with a pencil.

2 Check the height of the wall from ceiling to skirting, and then roll out the paper on your pasting table, and cut with scissors, allowing an extra 10cm on top of the length required. If it is very tightly rolled paper it may just roll itself up again once you cut it – in which case roll it back on itself the other way to keep it straight.

3 Paste the paper starting at one end, and make sure the paste goes over the edge of the paper, moving it around as necessary. If you position the edge of the paper at the very edge of the table it stops paste going onto the table (but still clean off any paste on the table before you prepare the next strip).

4 Gently fold both ends of the paper into the middle. This makes it easier to manage when carrying it and positioning it on the wall.

5 Some papers require that you leave them pasted for a certain amount of time before hanging so make sure you read, and stick to (not literally) this advice.

6 Carry the paper across to the chalk or pencil mark and unfolding the top, place it on the wall so that about 5 cm overlaps the ceiling. You will be surprised how easily the paper can be moved around into place at this stage, so don't panic about getting it dead on the line to start with. Use your flat palm on the paper to slide it so that it lines up perfectly with your chalk mark.

7 Then use the papering brush to brush down the paper, starting in the middle and working out to the edges, to help the paper stick to the wall and to remove any bubbles.

Keep the brush clean by wiping it regularly (on overalls is fine!) so that you don't start wiping paste all over the face of the paper. Now work your way down to the bottom of the paper, ensuring it remains butted up neatly to your line.

Remember to always keep your brush clean

8 Once it is in place and nicely flattened to the wall, use the tip of your scissors to crease the paper into the ceiling joint.

9 Then gently pull the paper away and use your scissors to cut along the crease.
Then brush it back into place and it should fit snugly to the ceiling. Do the same at the bottom along the crease with the skirting board.

You can use a knife to cut instead of scissors, but I find it's very easy to tear paper with a knife, so unless it's an intricate shape and this is the only option, it's better to use scissors.

Make sure you wipe any paste off the window frame, ceiling and skirting as you go along.

10 The next length you hang needs to be butted up neatly to the edge left by your first piece. Pay particular attention to sticking down the edges and push down firmly with your clean cloth to ensure they are stuck. If the paste has dried and they are not sticking well, pull the paper away gently, apply a little more paste and brush into place again, wiping away the excess paste.
If you need to match a pattern, make sure you cut the length according to the instructions for pattern repeats and line it up carefully on the wall before cutting the top and bottom.

11 Corners of the room can be tricky, so take your time. We were working on the external corner of our chimney breast. Measure the gap from the previous strip of wallpaper to the corner edge and then add 5cm. If you put one edge of the paper on the edge of your table, you can then use the hook edge of the tape measure to score along the line to be cut – making life easier.

12 Cut along the marked line and paste and position the paper in place, but leave the overlap unstuck.

13 Then mark a chalk line at the point where the small section needs to be pasted and paste the section into place and fold and paste down the overlap from the front section. Using overlap adhesive and a roller will help to achieve a smooth finish.

14 To turn an internal corner, mark a plumb line so that the next length of paper covers the overlap from the first wall. If the piece you trimmed off at the corner is wide enough, you can use it as your first length on the new wall.

If your room is wonky (as is the case in many older houses) allow 20cm extra on these lengths to allow for discrepancies and sloping ceilings and skirtings. It's advisable not to use patterned paper in such houses as it will highlight these problems and make matching more difficult for you.

Windows

1 When you get to the window, pattern match the length as normal and allow the paper to drop over the window recess, making sure the paper to the top and side of the recess is firmly stuck down. Make two horizontal cuts back to the corners, using the window sill as a guide for the bottom cut and the recess edge as a guide for the top.

2 Use scissors to make a series of right-angled cuts into the profile of the bottom corner of the sill. Then mould the paper around and under the sill to that the bottom half of the length can be positioned and trimmed.

3 Bend the flap of paper around and into the recess. Push the paper firmly into the wall and the window frame and trim all areas.

4 Cut the next length to extend from the ceiling, around the top of the recess to the top of the frame. Hang it overlapping the previous length, matching the pattern. Make a cut to the recess corner and tuck this under the recess and press into place.

5 Using a steel rule and a craft knife, make a manufactured butt join to cut a diagonal line through the area where the two pieces overlap. Make sure the line goes through the busiest part of the pattern to disguise the join.

6 Peel back the paper and discard the top section of the first length. Remove the bottom section of the new length and push the pieces back together to form a perfect butt join. Complete the other side of the window in the same way.

Sockets & switches

Light switches and plug sockets are not a major problem once you know how to deal with them. First turn off the electricity to the room, and loosen the light switch or socket away from the wall.

Then cut a diagonal criss cross in the paper once it is lying over the fitting. Cut away the middle of this in a square or rectangle

depending on the fitting you are working around. This will leave four little flaps which can be neatly tucked underneath the fitting before screwing it back on.

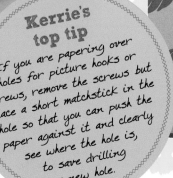

Kerrie's top tip
If you are papering over holes for picture hooks or screws, remove the screws but place a short matchstick in the hole so that you can push the paper against it and clearly see where the hole is, to save drilling a new hole.

FLOORING

It's all too easy to ignore the floor when you redesign your home, but your floor can have a powerful impact both visually and on your comfort. Floors can help insulate against cold, protect other rooms or neighbours from noise, provide waterproofing for wet rooms, non-skid surfaces to guard against accidents or extra resilience in areas of high traffic.

Here's where we explore all sorts of jobs related to floors, including laying them, repairing them and maintaining them. I haven't included carpets here, as most carpet purchases these days have free fitting included, which is well worth taking advantage of. Carpet laying is a tricky, skilled job so you really ought to get an expert to do it.

Laminate or solid wood flooring – you can fit what fits your budget

Wooden Floors

Real wood and wood-effect, or laminate, floors have exploded in popularity in the last 15 years. We'll look at laminate floors in the next section – here I am concentrating purely on real wood floors and floorboards.

It might be more expensive than laminate, but a real wood floor will last forever

When you look at floorboards it is easy to work out where the joists are and in which direction they run, because that is where the nails or screws holding down the boards will be.

Be aware that there are often pipes and cables in the cavity beneath floorboards, so use a detector before doing any drilling or nailing.

Kerrie's top tip

Small gaps between floorboards can easily be filled with papier-mâché, made from strips of newspaper and thick wallpaper paste. If you are not staining or re-varnishing mix some wood stain in to ensure a good match.

Squeaky boards

A common problem with older floors made of boards is that they start squeaking and creaking every time they are walked on – not great when you're trying to sneak in un-noticed after a late night with the girls! Squeaking is caused by one board rubbing against its neighbour, and is easily cured.

1 First drill a pilot hole through the board and into the joist below. (You can tell where the joists are positioned by the line of nails running along in the opposite direction to the boards).

2 Then screw the board to the joist in the offending area.

3 If you don't want to see screw heads, use a long nail rather than a screw, then use a nail punch to knock the nail head below the surface.

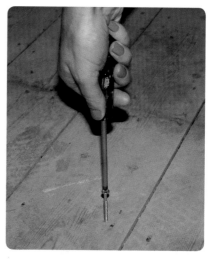

4 If this doesn't work, then dusting some talc into the joint can stop the squeak. If it still persists, then you may need to drive a small wedge of matching wood into the gap to create a snug fit.

Sanding

Sanding a floor is immensely satisfying, but be warned that it is hard work. Don't try and scrimp and do this with a hand sander – you will give up before you've done a square metre! Hire a floor sander (the hire company will provide you with all the necessary equipment, along with any consumables required).

www.hiretech.biz

* Make sure you wear a mask.
* Protect everything, including other rooms, from the inevitable mess and dust.
* Clear the entire floor area of all furniture before starting.
* Work your way around the room ensuring there are no protruding nails or other metal items (they can be knocked in with a nail punch).
* Tilt the sander backwards before you start it up as you should never have it running in a stationary position.
* Tuck the cable over your shoulder (as you should when mowing the lawn, incidentally) to make sure that you can't run it over.
* Sand along the line of the boards, not along the joists.
* Start with coarse sandpaper, and finish with fine.
* The edges and corners should be sanded with the edge sander, again following the length of the boards.

Staining or varnishing

Once you've finished sanding the floor you will need to ensure it's perfectly clean. The best way to do this is to vacuum all the dust up, then rub the floor down with white spirit to remove any remaining dust residue. Before starting, you may want to use wood filler on any holes, or insert wedges into any large gaps. Apply varnish thinly, and according to instructions on the tin in terms of minimum number of coats. As with the sanding, follow the line of the boards, which will mean following the grain of the wood. Be careful not to go over your previous brush strokes or it will leave a mark – working one board at a time can help avoid this. Make sure you work towards the door so that you can get out without walking all over your wet floor!

Preparation

If your floor is uneven you will need to level it before laying any flooring, including laminate floor, vinyl floor and tiles. As with all DIY jobs preparation is key and taking a short cut here would seriously compromise the finish, and quality of your floor.

It's worth spending time on the floor preparation for a better finished result

Boarding

Hardboard is usually sufficient as a base for most types of flooring, although if your floor is particularly uneven you may need to use thicker plywood. Lay the hardboard sheets smooth side up, in rows across the room. The easiest way to secure it is using a nail gun, but failing that hammering in nails is also effective but takes a bit longer. With each new row that you lay, stagger the joints so they don't line up with the previous row.

Plywood

Plywood is slightly harder to lay than hardboard. Ideally it should be screwed rather than nailed, and it's important to make sure your screws are long enough to go into the boards below, but not through them. Start in a corner of the room, and screw down the edges every 15cm. Then work along and across the board leaving 15cm gaps between screws to ensure it's tightly held down.

✳ In wet areas such as bathrooms it's advisable to use waterproof ply (known as marine ply) or waterproof MDF (known as green MDF). Plywood should be cut with a saw for straight lines; use a jigsaw to cut around pipes and odd shapes like the bottom of door frames.

Uneven floors

There is an easy way to see if your floor is uneven (if it's not already obvious). Lay your long spirit level on its side and lay a switched-on torch behind it. If you can see light under it, then it's uneven. Do this in several different places in the room. One warning – the floor level will be raised by preparation and the new surface, so doors will need trimming, but leave this until the final layer is in place.

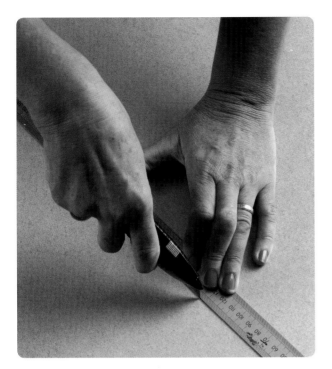

Hardboard

Hardboard is easy to cut – just cut a straight line on the smooth side of the board using a Stanley knife and your metal rule. Turn the sheet over, place the rule along the line and bend the board up, then use the knife to separate the two pieces of board.

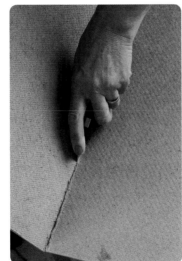

A nail gun makes light work of boarding

Concrete floors

A self-levelling compound should be used to level a concrete floor, and it isn't as hard or scary as it may sound. Start by sweeping the concrete floor thoroughly to ensure it's clean and dust free, then brush on a PVA glue solution to seal the floor. Once the PVA is dry, mix up the self-levelling compound according to instructions. Pour it onto the floor and allow it to settle to its own level. If necessary use a plastering trowel to level out any lumps and bumps, but be warned it dries fast so work quickly. Gradually work around the room in areas, again ensuring you end up by a door so you can get out!

self-levelling compound

work quickly as it dries fast

Laminate

Most laminate floors are tongue-and-groove – this means that they slot together and no glue is needed. We've used a click-style laminate which helps to get a perfect join each time. This is now the most common type of laminate flooring, and definitely the easiest to work with.

Before you start laying your flooring, you will need some extra tools that aren't included in the toolbox list from the first chapter. Firstly is a knocking block, which you need to push the boards together without damaging them. You will also need a jemmy, for pulling into place the last few boards where there isn't room to get a knocking block. The other item you'll need is a set of wedges, to help preserve the expansion gap around the edge of the room. You may well also need a jigsaw for awkward shapes around architraves.

Quantities

To calculate the number of packs you need to buy, first calculate your floor area. This is the length of the room (in metres) multiplied by the width, which gives you the number of square metres. Each pack of flooring will state how many square metres it covers, so a simple calculation of square metres divided by pack coverage will tell you how many packs to buy. Always add about 10 per cent to this total to cover mistakes and pieces that will need to be cut.

Underlay

Depending on the floor you have bought, you will need underlay. This may or may not include a damp proof membrane – be guided by the instructions. Membranes and underlays are very easy to lay and just need to be cut to size with a Stanley knife. They are essential for soundproofing purposes, as they act as a shock absorber.

Membrane
Standard foam underlay does not have a moisture barrier attached to it, so they should be used in places where there is no possibility of moisture coming out from the sub-floor.

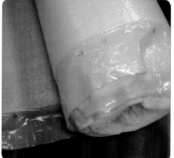

Damp proof membrane
This has an additional layer of moisture barrier attached to it, so is ideal if the subfloor is prone to damp.

Fibreboard Underlay
Natural insulating under floor panels for laminate flooring. The fibreboards offer sound reduction and helps eliminate unevenness in the sub floor making them ideal for use over wooden floor boards.

1 Once you have fitted any necessary underlay, start with a full plank in the corner of one wall, ideally the door wall. Make sure the tongue is facing the skirting board and pop some wedges in place to keep the board slightly away from the wall.

wedges will keep the board from the wall

2 Next place another plank end-to-end with the first plank. This will normally mean you need to tilt it into place where it should lock. You may need to put the knocking block on the other end of the second board and give it a tap to get it to lock together.

3 Continue along the room, across the doorway (leaving a wedge either side of the door, we'll come back to this in a minute) until you reach the end – where you will most likely need to cut a plank to the right size to fit the last section. When you measure, make sure you allow for the expansion gap. Fit the cut piece into position.

4 Begin the next row using the offcut from the plank you cut at the other end first. Continue to lay as before, putting the short edges together. Use the long edge of the previous row as a guide for alignment – but don't try fitting the long edges together at this point.

Gently push down using a tilted angle

5 Once the row is complete offer up the entire length to the previous row, using a tilted angle and gently push down. Use a zipper type action to move down the row until panels are level and flush. Having someone to help at this point will make life easier.

6 Before starting the third row, deal with the door area. This is important to do at this stage for ease, as you need to move the existing block of laminate floor away to fit it properly.

✳ Measure from the outer edge of each architrave, then deduct 12mm at each end for an expansion gap. Cut a board to this length.

Architrave

To obtain a professional finish around door architraves, it is a good idea to saw off the bottom of the architrave so that the flooring fits neatly under it. To measure how much to saw off, put a piece of underlay with a piece of flooring on top alongside the architrave and allow your saw to be guided by this.

Once the piece has been sawn off, and the laminate piece cut to the remaining profile of the architrave, slide the piece of laminate underneath into place.

8 Hold the board in position and mark with a pencil the shape of the architrave to cut out. Use a saw to cut this section out (or a jigsaw if necessary).

9 Now fit this strip into the existing two rows and slide back into position with the cut areas fitting under the architrave. If necessary you can hide any glitches around the architrave with a little bit of filler.

7 Now measure the width of the door gap from the existing plank, to just before the join with the flooring in the adjoining room. This is important as it will ensure the join in floors will be under the door and can be hidden by a threshold strip. Cut your laminate to this width (using a normal saw or a jigsaw).

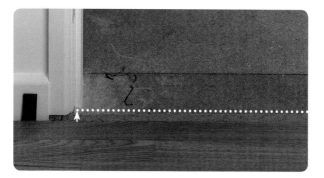

10 Once rooms are completed, a threshhold strip can be added to neaten everything off.

Threshhold strip between laminate and carpet

11 Continue adding boards throughout the room, following the same method outlined above.

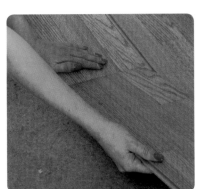

12 If you have other obstacles to cut around, such as pipes, mark the cut on your board in the appropriate place (depth and thickness).

* Drill a hole in the board big enough to fit the pipe through using a hole drilling drill bit.
* Then saw down each side of your markings to remove the section, but hang on to this bit of floor.

13 Now slide the plank into position and fix as normal, and use a little glue to stick the small piece into place behind the pipe. You could add a pipe cover around the base of the pipe to cover any small gaps.

14 When you reach the final row of board in the room, you will most likely need to trim the width of the boards to fit (remember to allow the 12mm expansion gap).

Finishing touches

You will also need to glue into place the beading around the edge of the room, which hides the expansion gap and gives it a tidy finish. Apply the glue to the edge touching the skirting, not to the floor – otherwise if there is expansion or contraction, the beading will just move with the floor, rather than stay in place and hide the gap. Make sure you use a mitre block to cut the corners that will fit together.

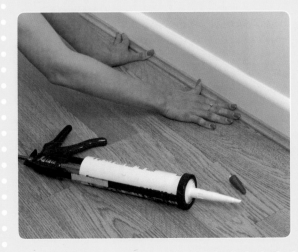

Floor tiles

Tiling is probably the most adventurous flooring option you can try yourself, but don't be put off as it's not as hard as it might sound, and with practice you'll quickly get into the swing of things. A few select tools such as a decent tile cutter and a profile gauge will make life a lot easier.

Warm-coloured floor tiles give a great mediterranean feel to a room

Surface preparation

It is crucial that the surface you are tiling on to is totally flat and stable – otherwise tiles will work loose or crack. Unless you have a flat concrete floor, the best option is thick plywood, (see page 68). Whatever the surface, you must first seal it using a PVA mix brushed on with a paintbrush.

You will need a fair amount of extra kit for tiling; don't try and scrimp or it'll be very hard work and you'll end up with a sub-standard end result. Here are the essential items:

Straight pieces of wooden battens to mark out your starting point and ensure a straight line. Tile cutter – you can use either a manual or electric one. The latter is more expensive but well worth the investment and it cuts right angles as well as straight edges. Tile file. Tile saw, for intricate shapes. Adhesive spreader. Grout float. Grout shaper. A profile gauge, if you don't already have one. Several clean cloths, sponges and buckets. Tiles, adhesive and grout (follow the guidelines given on the tile packs for quantity and type).

Tools for the job

1 Work out your starting point – ideally the centre of the room. Mark with a chalk or pencil line and screw your battens in place with short screws to give you a straight edge to tile against.

2 Apply enough adhesive for one tile directly to the floor. Use the adhesive spreader's corrugated edge so that you get a ridged finish and even coverage.

3 Place the tile onto the adhesive and press down firmly whilst wiggling the tile slightly into position right up against the batten, to ensure the adhesive spreads across the whole tile back.

4 Repeat the adhesive application in the next space along, and before laying the tile, add tile spacers to the end of the first tile to ensure an even gap between tiles.

✳ Continue down the row, and across the room in the same way laying all the full tiles and spacers (don't worry about the cuts around the edges just yet).

5 Keep wiping the tiles after each one is laid to remove any adhesive from the surface of the tile otherwise it will leave ugly marks.

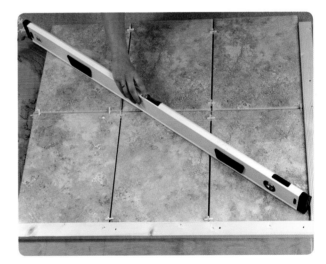

6 Use your long spirit level to check the tiles are flat. If one is raised, lift it, remove a little adhesive, re-lay it and check the level again.

✳ If a tile is lower than the others, lift it, add a little more adhesive, and re-lay it.
✳ You have a bit of time to play with before the adhesive dries to get the tiles positioned correctly and levelled.
✳ Once that's done, I would suggest leaving the room at this stage to dry overnight, before embarking on the cuts around the edges.

By day two, you will be feeling a lot more confident with your tiling ability, and you can start to see how the room will look once it's finished, which is always encouraging.

Cutting tiles

Since I have recommended you invest in an electric tile cutter, that's what I'm going to describe using, but if you haven't bitten the bullet and made this investment, then just substitute your cutting device.

1 Measure the gap between your first tile and the skirting, allowing for a grouting gap. Mark this out onto the back of your tile with a felt tip pen.

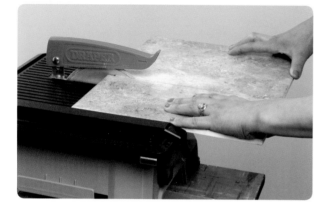

2 After reading the operating instructions of your electric tile cutter carefully – make sure you wear protective eyewear too – begin to cut the tile by pushing it gently towards the rotating blade.

3 You can then file the edges gently with the tile file to make them smooth. Before doing anything with adhesive, put the tile in place first dry to check that it fits, and adjust as necessary.

4 Then smooth adhesive onto the back of the tile itself – you'll find this much easier than trying to squeeze the adhesive into the gap on the floor.

5 Place the tile into position and wiggle it as before to ensure good adhesion. Continue around the room with all the straight cuts in the same way, always wiping off any adhesive from the tile surfaces, and still checking for levels.

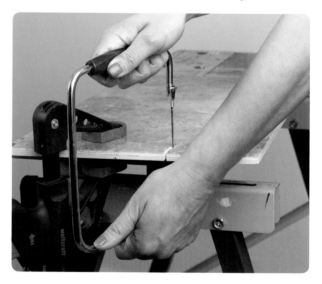

6 Finally, move onto the more intricate cuts around architraves and pipes etc. Here you may need to use your profile gauge to fit around the contours, and then use it as a guide to mark onto the face of your tile. Use a tile saw to cut around the marked line on the tile. Put adhesive on the back of the tile and wiggle into place as before.

A tile saw is useful

Grouting

1 You're nearly done. Depending on the tile type, they may need sealing before you grout. Either way, you must make sure the tiles are really clean, remove all the tile spacers, and then begin to apply the grout, working it right into the gaps between the tiles using your grout float.

2 As the grout starts to dry (but don't leave it too long) clean off the excess with a wet sponge. This is crucial to achieving a neat finish.

✳ You can shape your grout lines using a grout shaper, but I find a damp sponge whilst cleaning the tile works just as well and saves a bit of money on tools.

3 The final finishing touches such as threshold strips and pipe covers can now be applied.

✳ Stand back and admire your brilliant tiling. Well done!

Manual cutting

Using a manual tile cutter is a little harder than using an electric one. Place your marked tile to be cut into the cutter, with the line on the glazed side directly under the scoring blade. Run the scriber across the surface of the tile away from you to make an indentation along your line, then press the handle down to bring the snapper up and into contact with the underside of the tile. Gently press down to snap the tile in two – it should break evenly along the line you scored. If it doesn't, next time try scoring a little deeper.

Tiling a conservatory is a good place to start – plenty of straight edges!

Vinyl flooring

Vinyl flooring is perfect for kitchens and bathrooms as it is waterproof, durable and easy to clean. Some come with an anti-slip coating and others have extra cushioning which is great when your partner is standing for long periods of time doing the cooking and washing up…

styles of vinyl have greatly improved and can look like the real thing

Tools for the job

✻ Tape measure ✻ Marker pen ✻ Steel rule ✻ Stanley knife with ordinary blade and hook blade ✻ Building paper (or lining paper) ✻ 'Scribing' block (a chunk of 2x1 wood or similar parallel edge) ✻ Adhesive (either paste or tape – depending on subfloor) ✻ Sealant (if using vinyl in bathroom or kitchen)

Working with a paper template is the easiest and safest way of getting a good result. Flooring specialists can snip and tuck a vinyl floor into a room in a matter of minutes – but they've had plenty of experience. Follow the template formula shown here and you won't have any unwanted gaps.

Kerrie's top tip
Unroll the vinyl and put it as flat as you can in a warmish room for a few hours beforehand, as this makes it easier to cut and work with.

1 Roll out your first length of paper against a length of wall. If you are confident that it's a straight wall, then you can just butt the paper edge up against the wall/skirting edge.

2 Cut some squares out of the paper and stick masking tape across the opening to fix the paper to the floor. Do this all along the length to keep the template in position.

3 Position your next strip of paper for the other wall coming out from the corner. Cut the top of the paper at an angle, so you can easily stick it to the strip underneath. Continue to work around the room (see the relevant points below when you hit a difficult shape or pipework).

4 When you have completed the template – gently peel it away from the floor and stick it onto the top of the vinyl. Use your straight edge and a washable pen to mark the cutting line. Take advantage of any straight lines on your vinyl pattern as a good starting position. Use the straight blade for straight cutting lines and the hook blade for any curves. Press firmly but carefully as you cut – making sure your fingers are well out of the blade's way!

5 Use appropriate adhesive to stick the vinyl down. A paste is best for concrete screed (but you won't be able to lift the vinyl in the future). Double-sided tape is OK for wood subfloors.

6 If the vinyl is in a kitchen or bathroom, seal around all edges to avoid problems from steam and water.

Pipes

1 Tear out a small piece of paper from the main template around the pipe area. Position your ruler against the pipe and mark the outside edge of the ruler on the left, right and front of the pipe. Mark the inside edge behind the pipe (you may have to tilt the ruler at an angle to fit it behind the pipe).

2 When the template is positioned on the vinyl put the ruler against the lines on the template and mark off the inside edge of the ruler onto the vinyl. You will then end up with a square marked on the vinyl which will be the exact position of the pipe.

3 For standard 15mm pipe, mark around a 5p positioned in the centre of the square, then carefully cut it out (going around with short 'stabs' with a straight blade is easiest).

4 Cut two lines out from the circle to the edge of the vinyl, and remove the thin strip. Once the pipe is in position, this leaves a gap that can be filled with sealant and avoids any corners curling up when they get damp.

Odd shapes

A method the professionals use is 'scribbing' which initially sounds complicated, but once you 'get it', can produce accurate templates for all odd shapes in a room, including wonky walls. Have a few goes on a rough template first, so you get the idea.

1 Tear your paper template around the edge to be cut. Push a parallel edge up against the shape and mark a line along the opposite edge. Continue to do this at regular intervals around/along the shape.

2 Stick the template over the vinyl and put the parallel edge against a line marked on the template. Then mark the opposite edge onto the vinyl (using a washable pen). Do this for all the lines on the template and you will end up with an accurate cutting guide. You may have to curve off some of the edges by hand for certain shapes.

3 An alternative template method is to push the paper into or around the area to cut, creasing it into position and marking with a pencil. On curved shapes, cutting flaps above the line will help.

4 Once the vinyl is in position, seal any edges in kitchens or bathrooms.

www.karndean.co.uk

Practical but stylish. Vinyl is a great floor to have in a bathroom

Vinyl tiles

These are a very quick, effective and inexpensive way to finish your floor. The tiles have adhesive on the back, and you just peel off the backing and stick them in place. I say that's all you do – there is a little bit more to it than that, but it is very easy.

These look like real tiles but will be much warmer to walk on in bare feet!

The floor needs to be clean and sound before you start. You will need a profile gauge to copy the patterns of any intricate mouldings on to your tile in order to cut them to the right shape. The tiles are really easy to cut with a Stanley knife.

Before you start, lay the tiles out 'dry' (still with their backing on) to work out your starting point. Ideally avoid having small slivers on the sides or ends of the room. When you have decided where the tiles will go, mark out the edge of the first full row using our metal straight edge and a pencil. Now simply peel off

the adhesive backing of the first tile and place it neatly onto this line. Be accurate the first time as the adhesive doesn't allow for any movement once the tile is down. Then simply work down the line, butting the next tile tightly up to the first, then begin the next line, and so on.

Kerrie's top tip

When cutting intricate shapes in your vinyl tiles, try using sharp scissors rather than a Stanley knife – they are really easy to handle in comparison and give equally accurate results.

When it comes to the cuts at the edges, measure accurately and cut the tile accordingly before sticking. For architraves, pipes and so on, use the profile gauge and then trace the pattern onto the surface of the tile in pencil, before cutting.

The room can be finished with a threshold strip for neatness, and another trick is to run a small bead of silicone around the edge of the room, to cover any slightly less than perfect cuts at the edges and provide a more waterproof finish.

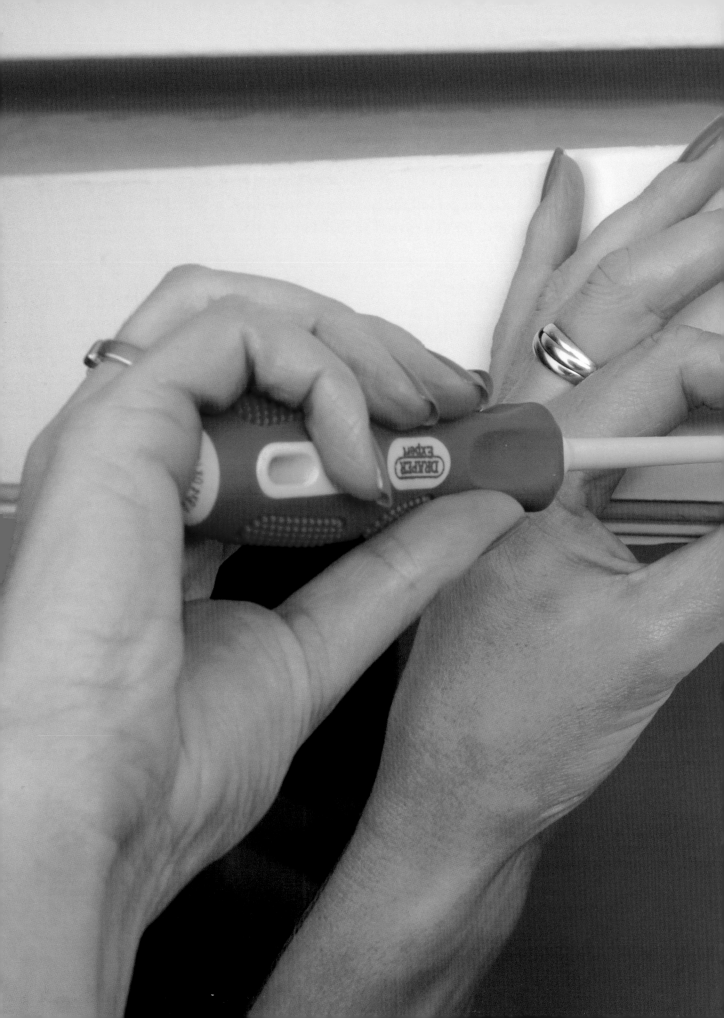

WINDOWS AND DOORS

Repairing windows and doors can seem a little daunting at first, but I promise there's nothing in here that you're not capable of. What's more, you can save yourself a lot of money by giving it a go yourself. When you've finished you can congratulate yourself on your new-found DIY skills by splashing out on that designer handbag or fetching new outfit – safe in the knowledge that your home is now more secure and they are less likely to be pinched! As well as making repairs to windows and doors, this chapter outlines ways in which you can enhance and improve the look and function of your existing fittings.

Once you've fitted locks, keep the key in a safe place

Curtain poles

This is one of those jobs that you've probably been nagging, I mean asking, your other half to do. Well take heart, it's quick and simple and you can definitely do it yourself, and you never know, he may even notice the new curtains the next time he comes into the room (but don't count on it!).

stylish curtains can finish off your decorating perfectly

Before starting, take a few minutes to work out the look you want. For maximum light, it's best to have a pole long enough so that when you pull the curtains open they sit against the wall either side of the window, rather than over the window itself. Also check the length of the curtain and therefore the height you can start above the window. As a general rule, the pole should be about halfway between the window recess and the coving or ceiling.

Add a decorative finial

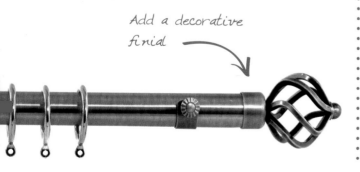

1 Measure above the recess with your tape measure, and mark in pencil the pole height above the window.

2 Using your long spirit level, draw a guide line from one side to the other. Two things to note here:

✱ The line might not be the same height above the window on both sides if your recess isn't level, but trust your spirit level, as it's important the pole is straight.

✱ Extend your pencil line to both sides of the window according to where you need the supporting brackets, as they are unlikely to be directly above the window itself.

3 Now work out the fixing height of the brackets along this line, so that the bottom of your curtain will hang where you want it, and the pole will line up with your pencil line – be careful not to line up the bracket bottom with this line for example, or your pole will actually be higher than you want.

4 Measure and mark the bracket position about 15cm from either side of the window recess, depending on the pole width and finished curtain width. The pole should extend a few centimetres past the brackets on either side.

5 Hold your bracket in position and mark the fixing holes, then drill pilot holes, insert the appropriate type of wall plug, and screw the bracket into place.

6 Put your pole into the brackets once you've put them all in place, and thread on the curtain rings, ensuring one is left outside the bracket.

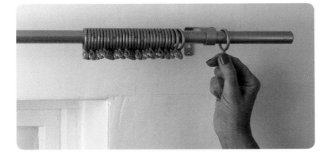

7 Finally, fix any decorative finial in place on the end of the pole.

Fixing a curtain track is very similar, although you may prefer to fix a wooden batten slightly longer than the track in the position you want the track first, and then fix the track to it.

Blinds

Roman blinds

Roman blinds are attached to a batten that is fixed to brackets above the window. Mark and screw brackets about 4cm in from each end of the blind. Then attach the blind to the brackets.

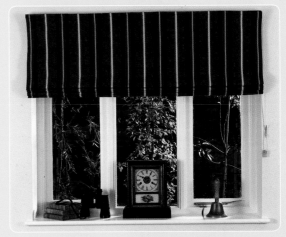

Roller blinds

1 Fix the brackets to the wall, checking the instructions to ensure that the left and right brackets are correctly placed.

2 Measure the distance between the brackets and if necessary saw the pole and cut the width of the blind to fit.

Replacing glass

If your other half has been careless with a football (and no doubt tried to blame it on your child… even if you don't have one), then you may well have a broken pane of glass to deal with. This is easy to do, but just be careful as you are dealing with broken glass and its obvious dangers.

Make sure you dispose of the broken glass carefully and safely

Whilst this appears a difficult job, it really isn't – but don't tell him that, and make sure you milk the guilt for all it's worth in massages and foot rubs!

Replacing windows

Before we get into the nitty gritty, there's one thing I think should be left to the professionals, and that's replacing whole windows. It's not that hard, but frankly it's not that easy either, and you're more likely to benefit from guarantees and warranties if you have them professionally installed. And make sure they have the British Standard Kite Mark too.

1 Start by putting on a pair of gloves and goggles and remove any loose pieces of glass. Use your screwdriver or an old chisel to get rid of all the old putty, remove all glazing springs (the little metal bits), clips or beading, and brush away any dust or dirt.

2 When all the old putty has been removed, gently remove any larger pieces of glass.

3 Tidy up the edges of the frame, removing any putty at the back (against the thin internal part of the frame).

4 My favourite bit comes next – mould the new putty in your hands until it's squishy and pliable (adding a bit of Polyfilla powder will stop it sticking in your hands). You'll need linseed putty for wooden frames, and metal casement putty for metal frames.

5 Then squidge a strip of putty around the recess, about 6mm thick. It doesn't have to be neat, as you'll tidy it up later.

6 You are now ready to fit the new pane of glass. Make sure it's the right grade and thickness, and is cut to 3mm smaller than the width and height of the opening. Most suppliers will cut glass to size for you, but if you do decide to do it yourself, you will need a glass cutter (small sharp tool) and your straight edge. You simply score across the glass, then lay it on top of the straight edge, press lightly with a hand on each side of the score, and it should break along the scored line.

Glass cutter

7 Press the glass into the putty, starting with the bottom edge then pressing forward. Never press the middle of the glass, always the edges, or you may break it.

8 Now you will need to put new glazing springs in place to hold the piece of glass – but make sure you knock these in with the side of an old chisel rather than a hammer, for obvious reasons!

9 Run another strip of putty in the angle created between the new glass and the frame.

10 Use a putty knife to smooth the putty and make the corners neat. Copy the existing putty's angle to give a better, even-looking finish. The trick is to smooth the edge down in one sweep and then flick the excess off. If you don't get it right first time, just replace the putty and have another go. Now go indoors and use your putty knife to remove the squished out putty on the other side of the window.

11 Give the window and frame a clean with a cloth soaked in methylated spirit to clean off any excess putty and fingerprints. In two weeks the putty can be painted, but not before as it may shrink and crack.

Fitting a door

This is a slightly more complicated job than it may seem – or at least it is if you want to do it right and have a door that fits well. However, if you follow this step-by-step guide, you can't go wrong … and it is a job that you can do on your own, with a few tricks of the trade.

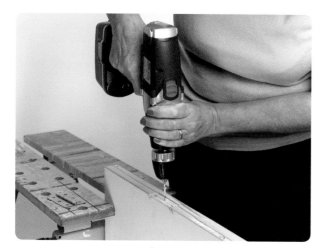

Doors are a crucial part of your home … and not just for slamming dramatically to make your point in an argument with your other half!

Internal doors help to keep heat in a room and can stop, or at least delay, the spread of fires and external doors are crucial to maintain the security of your home – so it is important that they are all well-fitted and maintained. I'll explain below how to solve some of the common problems with doors and also how to replace them.

Kerrie's top tip

If you are hanging a door, your best friend is an old paperback book! You can use this under the door to support it to the exact height that you require by adding or taking away pages.

1 The first step is to ensure the new door has a 3mm gap all the way around it – top, bottom and both sides. If necessary, cut and plane as described in the sticking doors panel.

2 Once your new door is the right size, position it (using the top tip to ensure the gap is correct at the bottom), and mark on it the exact position of the old hinges.

3 Lie the door on its side and position the hinges on these marks, drawing a line all the way around them, including marking the depth of the hinge onto the front edge of the door.

4 Use your chisel to make a cut at each end of the hinge position, very slightly outside the line edge. Then chisel along the side of the pencil line, cutting to the depth of the hinge.

5 Remove the marked wood with a chisel, taking care not to split the wood. Making slots along the wood as shown will make this easier.

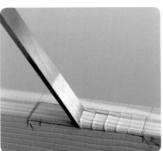

6 Gently use the chisel blade to remove the wood from the front edge, to the depth of the hinge.

7 Hold the hinge in place, mark the screw holes.

8 Drill small pilot holes and then screw the hinges firmly into place.

Make sure the screws are tightened well

Sticking doors

A door will stick when the edges of it rub against either the frame or the floor. Either way this is very easy to solve.

∗ If the door is sticking on the edge, mark with a pencil where the door is catching the frame, then open the door and plane the edge where the mark is. Just do a little at a time, and keep closing the door to check. It is easy to plane more if you need to – it's very hard to fill a gap if you've planed away too much!

∗ If the door is sticking against the floor, measure the height you need for good clearance – 3 mm is usually about right. Find or cut a small piece of wood to this height, then use the block to guide your pencil along the bottom of the door to make a mark. You will then need to remove the door and cut it either with a saw or a plane.

∗ Once you've trimmed your door, side, top or bottom, make sure you prime the wood (see Chapter Three) before repainting.

9 Now position the door in the doorway and secure the other half of the hinges on to the door frame. If you don't have someone to help you hold the door, read the top tip.

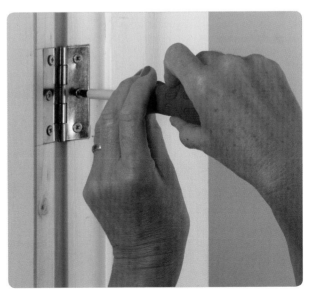

Door handles

This is a precise job – take your time to get it right so your door will close snugly. A new handle on a door can really transform the look of an old tired door, especially if you're upgrading from a tired brass door knob to a funky chrome handle.

You can match handles to the colour of your light and socket fittings

Check any information that comes with a new hollow door, as there are specific sides and positions for fixing locks and handles.

Kerrie's top tip

When working on a door use a wedge to keep the door fixed firmly, especially when you are drilling.

1 Line up the new latch case (the bit that will go inside the door) with the existing strike plate on the door frame, and mark the top, bottom and end onto the door with a pencil.

2 Run the lines around the side of the door, and then draw a vertical line through the middle (this will show you where to drill later).

3 Measure where the spindle centre of the latch case is and mark this on the door too.

4 Select a flat drill bit that's slightly larger than the latch case and put a bit of electrical tape around the drill bit's stem to mark the depth of the hole needed to fit the latch case.

5 Drill into the door using the vertical guideline you drew, and keep drilling until the electrical tape touches the door. It's important to be precise with this. You also need to drill both sides of the door on your spindle marking, but make sure you change to a smaller drill bit first (but one that is larger than the actual spindle).

6 Put the latch case into the hole you've drilled, make sure it's perfectly vertical, and mark the top and bottom, then chisel out the wood within your guide lines to the depth of the latch plate.

7 Push the latch into position, drill pilot holes and screw into place.

8 Insert the spindle through the latch (it may need cutting down in size) and then put the handles onto the spindles. Make sure they are absolutely vertical, and mark the screw holes with your bradawl.

9 Screw the handle into place, but use your hand-held screwdriver as otherwise you may slip and damage the handle.

＊ Check that the door engages correctly, and if necessary move the latch plate on the door frame.

Hinge fixings

A door may not shut properly because the hinge fixings are loose. Sometimes this can be resolved simply by tightening the screws, but if the screws are loose then you'll need to do a slightly more complex repair.

1 Remove the door and drill out the screw holes to the size of a wooden dowel.

2 Rub dowels in wood adhesive and hammer them into the holes until they are flush. You can trim any excess dowel with a chisel and hammer. Wipe away any excess adhesive.

3 When the glue is dry, hold the door back in position and mark the hinge screw holes (you'll need some help here). Drill pilot holes into the dowels where your marks are.

4 Reposition the door and screw the hinge into place, using new screws if the old ones were damaged.

Window locks

Windows are a vital part of our homes, providing light, ventilation and views – however they can also be a weak spot in terms of heat loss and security, so here are a few tips for getting your windows into tip top condition and keeping them that way.

Adding additional locks may help with your home insurance costs

Window locks should be fitted to any easily accessible ground floor windows – and this should also help to reduce your home insurance premium. Depending on your window type (sash, casement, UPVC etc) there are many different types available – though if you have UPVC windows check with the manufacturer that adding locks will not invalidate your guarantee.

Kerrie's top tip

Window locks are a great idea for security, but remember that you might need to get out in a hurry – for example if there is a fire – so keep your window keys somewhere easily and quickly accessible.

Casement

There are two main choices here – a stay lock which allows you to lock the window ajar to allow ventilation as well as fully closed, or a standard lock which only locks the windows when shut.

A standard casement lock has two parts – a striking plate and a locking body. The plate should be located on the fixed frame and the locking body should be on the opening casement section. Here's how to fit one.

1 Close your window and use a pencil to mark the position where you want the lock. Use your bradawl to mark the points you need to drill.

2 Then drill small pilot holes for the screws, but make sure the holes are not as big as the screws or they won't tighten.

3 Screw the locking body into place on the opening casement.

4 Then fix the striking plate in place on the frame.

5 Check the lock works smoothly with the special key it comes with, and if not, then adjust the position of the striking plate.

The alternative fixing for a casement window is a stay lock – which fits under the stay and locks it in place. It is usually sufficient to replace one of the existing stay pins, but you can do both if you prefer. Remove the stay pin and place the new stay lock pin in place, put the stay down onto it, and mark with a bradawl where to drill. Carefully drill pilot holes (smaller than the screws) then screw the new stay lock pin into place, close the stay, and position the locking nut on top using the key provided with the lock.

Sash windows

There are various options for locking sash windows; one type goes through both parts of the closed window, which also helps to stop draughts. Other types are shown below.

1 This fixes to the horizontal part of the windows and the key undwinds a small bolt which prevents the window catch from opening.

2 These stay locks are ideally fitted both sides of the window on the vertical edge. The ones shown need to be fixed flush with the wood. You lock them by using the key to twist out the barrel which then prevents the window from being lifted.

Kerrie's top tip

If fitting sash window stay locks, opt for two. Fit one retainer just above the bottom sash to keep the window tightly locked, then place the second one a few inches higher. This means that you can have the sash window open a few inches whilst still maintaining security, as it can't be pushed open any higher.

Door locks

Door locks provide perhaps the most important security aspect of your home so it is essential that they work properly so that you don't get shut in during an emergency and so that uninvited guests can't get in easily and pinch all your Jimmy Choos when you're out (although in fairness they would at least be exhibiting good taste).

You don't need to get the pros in if you just want to change the locks

Changing a cylinder lock

1 Unscrew the lock body. Hold on to this as you'll need to put it back on afterwards.

2 Unscrew the two retaining screws but hold the cylinder part in place, and leave the mounting plate in position too.

3 Remove the old cylinder from the outside and slide the new cylinder immediately into place and replace the screws.

Kerrie's top tip
Make sure you've bought the correct size replacement lock as depths differ. Standard depths are 2.5in and 3in.

4 The strip in the new cylinder may need cutting down to the size of the original. You can now replace the lock body and check that the door closes and the lock works properly.

Choosing a lock

Approximately 40% of domestic burglars gain access from the front or back door, so make sure your doors are as secure as possible. If you'd rather not tackle these jobs, it's worth getting someone in to do them. Make sure the locks have the 'kite mark' and are passed to the British Standard BS3621. An exterior door should ideally have at least a 5 lever lock, but additional mortice bolts and hinge bolts are worth adding. If you are fitting a cylinder lock to an exterior door, make sure it's a deadlocking one.

Changing a 5-lever lock

1 This is a simple job. Remove the handle on the inside by unscrewing it, and put it to one side to put back later.

2 Remove the spindle bar but hang on to this too as you'll need it later.

3 Unscrew the lock section and remove – you can help it on its way by putting your screwdriver in the spindle hole and pulling it towards you.

4 Fit and secure the new lock into place (you may need to chisel away a little more wood to ensure a snug fit. Replace the spindle and the handle and check that the lock works.

Fitting a mortice bolt

1 Mark the position you want the bolt on the door edge then using a square edge mark across the top and bottom line where it will fit.

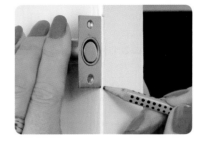

2 Use your tape measure to find the centre of each line and mark this, then join them with a vertical pencil line between the two horizontal lines. Then draw a cross from one corner to the other so that you can find dead centre.

3 Drill using a flat drill bit to the depth recommended on the packaging.

4 Insert the bolt and hold it in place whilst you mark around it the area that will need to be chiselled out to allow it to sit flush.

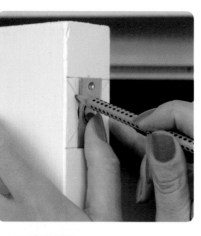

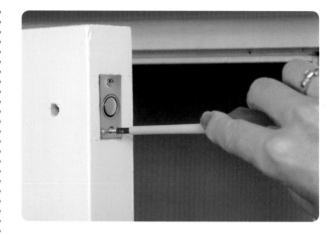

5 Chisel out the marked area so that it will fit flush. Take time over the chiselling and practise on some spare wood if necessary.

8 Drill pilot holes for the bolt and screw it into place. Make pilot holes for the key plate then screw that into place.

6 Hold the bolt against the inside of the door and mark the position of the keyhole with a pencil or bradawl.

9 Check that the key works.

Keep the key somewhere safe!

10 Mark and drill a hole for the bolt in the door frame and fix the mortice plate.

Fix the mortice plate

7 Drill a hole through just as far as the bolt hole, not all the way through the door.

Other problems

Draughts

Doors and windows are some of the main areas of your home that can let in draughts. Dealing with these can save you money on the heating bills – but be careful to ensure you still have sufficient ventilation, especially if you have a solid fuel fire, a gas fire or a boiler with an open flue.

Doors can be fitted with a brush draught excluder on the bottom of the door or an external draught excluder. You can also buy things called 'escutcheons' which are basically a set of two fixings, an open one to go over a keyhole on the outside of a door, and one with a cover plate to go on the inside.

Finding a draught

To check if you have draughts (if it's not obvious where they're coming from) hold a lighted candle near the window and move it around the edges to see where it begins to flicker. If the draught is coming from between the window and the wall, then a simple bead of silicone sealer will do the job. If the draught is coming from the space between the window and the frame, which is a lot more likely, then stick a strip of self-adhesive foam insulating strip around the inside edge of the frame when it's open, then shut the window and it should be a snug fit. You can buy the foam strip, usually wrapped in a spiral, in any DIY store.

Sticking windows

Sticking sash windows are common; it's normally caused by over-painting, in which case they need to be stripped and repainted. The sticking may also be caused by swelling of the wood, in which case they will need planing. The hard bit is getting the window open in the first place. Your best bet is to tape up the glass first to stop it from breaking, then use a wooden block against the frame and gently tap it with a mallet to break the seal, repeating the process all around the frame. If it still doesn't budge, try tapping a scraper down the window edge to release the two painted surfaces.

A casement window sticking is normally caused by stiff hinges, loose hinges or too much paint, all of which are easily solved once you work out which one is the problem. In order, solve it by lubricating with WD40 spray, tightening screws or stripping back paint.

Rattling

Sash windows can be prone to rattle as they age, because the beadings move and shrink. You have three options – first, you can shove a wedge of wood between the sashes, which will stop the rattle but not really solve the problem. Second is to fit a nylon pile draught excluder between the sash edges and the beadings, which will bulk it out and stop the rattle, as well as providing better insulation. But if the problem persists, the third option is best, which is to move the beadings – however, this is a tricky job best left to a professional joiner, or you might end up with a worse problem than you started with.

PLUMBING

Dealing with water and plumbing sounds scarier than it is – with a little careful planning and knowledge, you'll be amazed at what you can achieve, how much you can save, and above all, how good it will make you feel that you did it yourself! In this chapter we will explore how to do some simple maintenance tasks such as bleeding your radiators to make your central heating more effective. We will also cover how to unblock a sink or toilet, which whilst not pleasant, will certainly save you a fortune. We will also look at how to get that drip out of your life – though sadly just the tap variety, the other is down to you! You will also learn how to fix problems with your toilet cistern, how to manage a leaky pipe and finally how to install a dishwasher or washing machine.

Get rid of those drips – just follow the instructions in this chapter

Leaking taps

This is one annoying drip that you can change (you'll need a different book if you have the other kind…). The only tools you will need are an adjustable spanner, your flat head screwdriver, and a clean cloth to protect the tap from scratches.

A dripping tap could waste as much as 90 litres of water a week

The reason your tap is leaking is most likely because the washer or valve is worn, or if it's a kitchen tap, it may be a worn O ring. These are all easily fixed. You can tell what kind of tap you have by how far round you can twist the handle – if it's just a quarter turn, then it's a ceramic disk type tap, if it rotates further, then it's most likely a rubber washer. You will probably need to dismantle the tap first to see what you need to buy to repair it, unless you have a stock of replacements (dads often do, so it's worth asking!).

Kerrie's top tip

When working on a tap or above a sink or bath always put the plug in, in case you drop a small part or screw into the sink. Trust me – I learnt this one the hard way.

Getting into your tap

1 The first thing you need to do is turn off the water supply. Look under the sink below the taps and hopefully you'll find an isolation valve – a simple valve with a screw set into it that you twist a quarter-turn with a flat head screw driver. If the slot is running in line with the pipe the water is on, if it is horizontal to the pipe, the water is off.

2 Once you've turned it off, turn the tap on just to remove any water in the pipe and to check that the water is turned off properly. If you don't have isolation valves on your pipes, you will need to work backwards through your system to the main stop cock – this will usually be under your kitchen sink, and will turn off all the water in the house rather than just the tap you're working on. Again, run the tap to remove any standing water and to check that the water is off.

3 To gain access to the inside of the tap, you need to access the handle screw – this is normally hidden under a cap on the handle, and the cap is usually easily removed using a flat head screw driver (be careful not to scratch the tap).

unscrew to gain access to the disk or valve

4 As you remove parts of the tap, lay them out in the order they came off, so you can put it back together correctly again afterwards. On single lever taps you will most likely need to flip off the hot and cold insert to get access to the screw. Your tap may differ slightly from what I've described here, but usually it will be pretty evident how to get inside – if in doubt, though, you may need to contact the manufacturer, check on the internet to see if there's a diagram or online advice, or even get someone in to help you.

Line up the parts as you go

Disk valve

Replacing a ceramic disk should be an easy task, as you just dismantle your tap and remove the whole valve, take it along to your local DIY store or plumbers' merchant and they'll supply you with a new replacement valve. However, unless you can go back to where the original tap came from, you may need to search further for a replacement valve as there are so many taps on the market, stores often no longer stock the spare parts. It's worth checking out larger companies, such as Bristan (www.bristan.com) as they have a spare parts service.

Traditional tap

1 Replacing a rubber washer is really simple. Take the handle cap off and remove the screw as outlined above. There may also be a sheath covering the valve, which you should remove and keep to one side with the handle and screw. The valve is likely to be copper-coloured.

2 Use your spanner to loosen the valve so that you can remove it.

3 You will then find the washer on the bottom part of the valve. If there is a nut in place – remove it. The washer can be removed using a flat head screwdriver, or often just by hand. Replace the washer with one of an identical size and thickness – this is really important to prevent further leaks.

4 To reassemble the tap simply put the bits back together in reverse order, being careful not to over-tighten the valve.

Kitchen tap

Kitchen taps tend to have a single spout, although you may also have a tap like this in your bathroom.

1 The likely cause of a leak is the O ring, so this will need to be replaced. There is a small grub screw behind the spout, at the bottom (I bet you'd never noticed that before!). Undo the screw and lift the spout off. You may need to use an angled screwdriver.

2 The O ring will be visible on the base of the spout. You will probably have to use your flat head screwdriver to get the O ring off, as they are very tight, and if necessary cut it off. Replace the O ring by rolling on a new one,

and then replace the spout. Once you are happy everything is reassembled, turn the water back on to check, and if necessary adjust the tap. If you've fixed a washer and the tap is still leaking, it may be the O ring on the body of the valve, so check this for wear and tear and replace it if necessary.

Dishwashers & Washing Machines

Both machines are very similar to install, so the method described below applies to both and presumes that you already have pipes in place. As with any work involving water and taps, ensure the water is turned off before you start anything.

Your new machine will come with its own supply hoses which will eventually run from the back of the machine to the fixed pipes on the wall; there will be a blue one which connects to the cold water, and there may be a red one (not all machines have this) which connects to the hot water. You will also need some slip joint pliers, a jubilee clip and a flat head screwdriver. If there isn't an existing access hole in your kitchen cupboard, you will also need a drill with a hole saw attachment so that you can feed the waste through to your sink waste pipe.

There are two main elements that need connecting – the water coming in and the waste going out of the machine. Decide on the position of your machine on this basis – ie within reach of supply pipes already in situ on your wall (including hot if your machine needs a hot feed) and of the waste pipe

We can only show you how to install one type of dishwasher

under the sink. The supply pipes will normally already have connection points with isolation valves on them, with a blue valve for denoting cold and red for hot. If your pipes do not have connection points, then you will need to have them installed by a plumber (unless you're brave enough to attempt pipe cutting and possibly soldering, which isn't rocket science, but it's a bit too fiddly to go into here).

The waste hose can connect in two ways, either directly to the sink waste (which I'll explain here) or into an upright waste pipe already in place. The latter is really simple and you literally just place the waste hose into the top of the pipe and clip it into place.

Connecting

1 Most modern sink traps have adaptor points already in place to attach appliance waste hoses to. Simply unscrew the stop cap.

2 Then screw on your adaptor, being careful not to overtighten it (brute force isn't everything!).

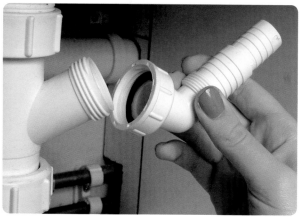

3 Feed the waste hose from your machine through the hole in the side of the cupboard. If this doesn't exist, you'll need to attach a suitable hole saw to your drill and make one in the top area of your cupboard side.

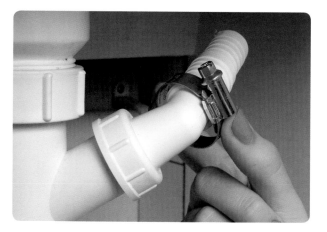

4 Put a loose jubilee clip onto the adaptor, then place the waste hose onto the adaptor as far as it will go.

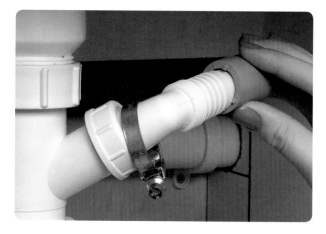

5 Slide the jubilee clip over the waste hose and tighten it using your flat head screwdriver. Connecting your supply hoses is easy – and a job where slightly more delicate female fingers come in handy.

6 Start at the machine end and, once you've checked the washer is still in place, gently twist the connector into place, being careful not to cross-thread it as it will leak if you do. Then use your slip joint pliers to tighten the connection, but not too tight.

7 Then do the same at the supply pipe end, but if you are not using the hot water feed, it's a good idea to add a cap.

8 Start by hand and then tighten using your pliers. Repeat this process for the second hose, if there is one.

use your slip joint pliers

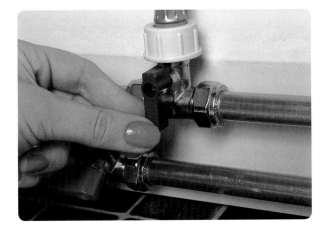

9 Then you're ready to turn the water back on, so simply twist the isolator valve(s) on to start the feed. Check for leaks at all points where you've joined pipes or hoses, and ideally the first time you run your machine, do it whilst it's still pulled out from the work surface so you can keep an eye on the back for any leaks. Once you're happy it's all working well, slide it into place under the work surface, being careful not to kink any hoses in the process as this could cut off the flow of water.

Those codes

While we're on the subject of washing machines – if like me, you've filed your machine instructions away and always wonder what half the symbols are on your clothes when you come to wash, iron or dry them – here's a quick reminder.

 The wash tub indicates the most appropriate programme for that particular fabric.

 The maximum temperature is shown in °C. These will be 95, 60, 50, 40 or 30°C. In addition to the temperature a bar may be present below the wash tub symbol.

Where there is no bar below the wash tub maximum agitation is recommended. This symbol appears on robust fabrics such as cotton and linen.

 Where a single bar is shown beneath the wash tub, the washing action (agitation) should be reduced. This symbol is found on more delicate fabrics such as poly cotton, acrylics and viscose.

 A broken or double bar beneath the wash tub symbol shows that only the most gentle wash action is required, as the fabric is likely to contain washable wool or silk.

The wash tub symbol with a cross through it means that the fabric is not suitable for washing.

 Where a hand is shown in the wash tub, the garment may be hand washed but should not be machine washed.

 Chlorine bleach may be used.

Do not use chlorine bleach.

The letter within the circle advises the dry cleaner which type of solvent can be used.

A circle with a cross means that the garment is unsuitable for dry-cleaning.

One dot = Cool
Two dots = Warm
Three dots = Hot

Cross = Do not iron

The information shown in the square gives the recommended drying method for that fabric.

Today many fabrics can be tumble-dried and this is indicated by a circle within the square. The most suitable heat setting for the garment is indicated by the addition of 'dots' within the circle.

One dot indicates low or half heat is required – normally synthetic fabrics.

Two dots indicates high or full heat is required – normally cotton fabrics.

A cross within the circle, or across the square indicates that the garment should not be tumbledried.

Sinks & drains

This isn't the most glamorous job on the list, but it is a really useful skill to master and it will also teach you to prevent the blockages you may have inadvertently caused in the past by pouring cooking oil down the kitchen sink, or allowing stray hair to clog up the bath outlet.

Invest in a plug strainer in the kitchen and clear hairs from bath plug holes

Depending on what's blocked and how badly, the main kit you will need comprises cloths, goggles and gloves (and possibly a face mask if you're sensitive to smells!), a plunger, a bucket or bowl, and a nifty gadget called an auger.

There are various chemical products on the market which you can use to try and dislodge your blockage – but be extremely careful and don't mix products. There was a terrible article in the paper about a lady who tried one product which didn't work, so she tried another – and the resulting mixture caused a reaction inside the pipe which then ruptured and covered her in corrosive chemicals. Not nice, so be warned.

Manually unblocking a sink is straightforward. If using a chemical cleaner has failed, you need to resort to brute force/woman power!

Unblocking a sink

1 First of all, block the overflow with a cloth to create a vacuum, then put your plunger over the plug hole and, holding it in place, move it up and down. This should dislodge the blockage. If that doesn't work, repeat the process a few times. If it still doesn't work, then the blockage may be further down the pipe.

2 Place your bowl under the waste pipe, and unscrew the U-shaped plastic pipe section. Clear any blockage you find in this section and replace it (but remember not to use the tap above to clean it out – easily done but not advisable!)

3 Some sinks may have a 'bottle' trap, but once unscrewed, the procedures are the same.

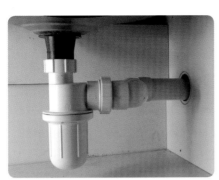

4 If you haven't yet found the blockage, you'll need to work further back down the pipes. Unscrew the next section of pipe (the main part of the 'trap') so that you get easier access to the main waste pipe.

5 Then use the auger to clear the blockage. Pull out around a metre from the auger and tighten the screw so that it doesn't recoil. Push the coiled end into the pipe until you feel and dislodge the blockage.

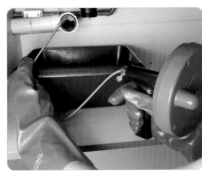

Blocked toilet

Unblocking a toilet is probably the least pleasant job I'm going to describe, but it's a necessary evil. However, I promise to make it quick and painless, and you don't need photos for this! As with sinks, first try a chemical cleaner, following instructions carefully. If this fails, use the auger in the same way described above for the pipe unblocking, and again be very sure to thoroughly disinfect it afterwards, and allow it to dry before winding it back in.

Rubber gloves are essential – colour is optional

6 Once done, reassemble the trap, ensuring all rubber washers are in place correctly. If any washers are worn or damaged, it's wise to replace them. Run the tap to ensure it's clear and there are no leaks. Take care to disinfect the section of auger you used, and allow it to dry before coiling it back into its casing.

Damaged washers should be replaced

Cisterns

Just what you've always wanted – a lesson on loos. Get to know the inside of yours so you know what's where if there's a problem. Check if you have an overflow pipe on an exterior wall or if the overflow runs back into the pan.

Cistern problems

✱ If your overflow pipe is dripping, and the arm of your ballcock is metal, you can gently bend it down slightly, so that the water flow is cut off before the overflow level is reached. If the arm is plastic, you can adjust it.

✱ If the water flow stops, then there might just be a problem with the ball float getting stuck on the edge of the cistern. Turn the mains water off, flush the loo and adjust the valve arm so that the ball doesn't rub against the edge of the cistern in any height position. Turn the water back on and check if the cistern fills properly before replacing the cover.

✱ If the overflow pipe is flowing more profusely, gently raise the ball with your hand and if the water flow continues, you'll need to replace or repair the valve (see below and opposite).

✱ If there's a grumbling noise when you flush the loo, your cistern valve either needs dismantling and cleaning out (due to a build up of debris/lime scale) or changing. Again, follow the procedures opposite.

Leaking valve

Sometimes all that's needed to fix a leaking valve is a new washer. The modern type of valve shown opposite uses a diaphragm washer. Repair kits are also available for the older types of valve (usually brass). A good hardware shop will usually stock both types.

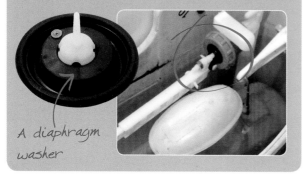

A diaphragm washer

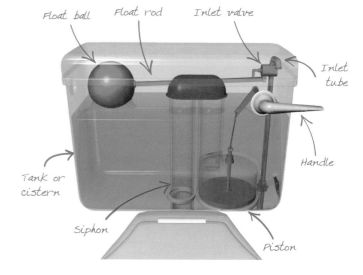

Float ball   Float rod   Inlet valve   Inlet tube   Handle   Piston   Tank or cistern   Siphon

When you press the handle, a lever inside the tank pulls the piston up, forcing some water through the siphon. This provides suction in the siphon, and the rest of the water follows, emptying the tank.

The tank empties quite quickly, and the float ball floats to the bottom. That means the float rod is no longer pressing against the valve, so water begins to flow into the tank, filling it up again.

Replacing a valve

1 Turn off the mains water and flush the loo. Remove the ballcock by twisting it off the arm of the valve.

4 Remove the pipe – but have a bowl underneath to catch any remaining water.

5 Unscrew the other nut which will be holding the cistern valve in place and lift the unit out of the cistern.

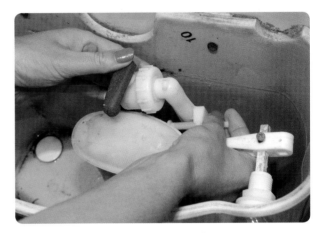

2 Scoop out any remaining water with a cup. Then mop the rest out, along with any dirt or loose particles, with a cloth or sponge.

6 Make sure you have bought the same replacement fitting as the original (side, bottom or top entry). Follow the instructions with your new valve. You can adjust the arm once the ball float is fitted so there is room for movement in the cistern.

3 Use an adjustable spanner to loosen the nut that links the cold water feed into the cistern.

Other problems

Plumbing can open up plenty of 'opportunities' for DIY. Here are a few more straightforward tasks you can do yourself (but if you want to take on some bigger projects, look out for the Haynes Plumbing Manual which will be published in 2012).

Pipes

Noisy Pipes

Most pipes which carry hot water will make a noise as they expand and contract and there isn't much that you can do to prevent it. A build up of scale if you live in a hard water area can also cause noise. If you are able to precisely locate the problem area, then spraying expanding foam under the pipe can help prevent or at least muffle the noise. If your pipe makes a loud banging noise when the water has just been turned off, this is known as water hammer. The cause of this is actually back at the point of the tap and is most likely a worn washer – and you already know how to deal with that.

Frozen Pipes

If your pipes have frozen, turn off the main stopcock and drain the system. Apply a temporary repair as explained opposite, and then partly open the stopcock and apply heat using a hair dryer (never a naked flame), starting by the tap and working backwards down the pipe.

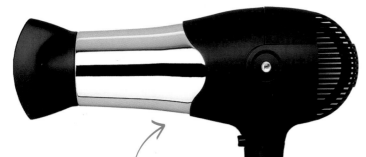

Use this on your frozen pipes first, then do your hair!

Leaking Pipes

There are many causes of a leaking pipe, there may be a break because the pipe has corroded, or frozen, or possibly even where a DIY accident has taken place with a misplaced nail (though of course this wouldn't be your doing, as you'd always use your detector before drilling or nailing wouldn't you?). You need to act fast to prevent damage to flooring or ceilings below. Firstly turn off the water supply to the area and dry the outside of the affected pipe. You can carry out a temporary repair so that you can continue to use water, but you should also call a plumber to replace the affected area.

To repair a small hole, push the tip of a pencil into the hole as far as you can and snap it off. Dry the pipe with a cloth and then wind waterproof tape around and around the pipe to bind it. If the problem with the pipe is a small fracture then just use waterproof tape tightly wrapped around to seal it. If the fracture is larger and more like a crack, then apply epoxy glue all around the pipe before you bind it with tape. Now call a plumber!

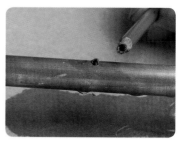

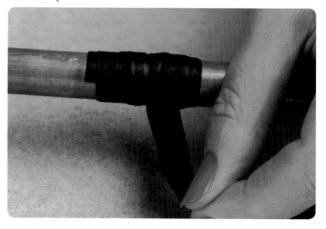

Radiators

Your radiators should be bled at least once a year – and immediately if the top of your radiators feel cool, or gurgle when the heating's on. Bleeding removes air from the system. This not only helps the heating to be more effective, but will also prevent corrosion on the inside of the heating system, which can lead to major problems down the line if left untreated. It will normally be

You need a radiator key to bleed your radiator

the radiator at the top of your system that is worst affected, but it's a good idea to check and bleed them all, and it's a very simple process. The only equipment you will need is a cloth and the radiator key. Hold the cloth under the valve at the top of the radiator and use the key to very gently loosen the valve nut in an anticlockwise direction. Do not remove it completely.

Use a cloth to prevent drips marking the floor

You will hear air escaping as soon as it's open far enough, so there is no need to turn it further. Once all the air has escaped, water will follow, so as soon as this happens, tighten the nut back up again, and then repeat the process with the next radiator. Be quick and careful here – you don't want a squirt of dirty water on your new cream carpet. If the water that comes out is rusty or sludgy then you need to have your system drained and flushed. This is a simple job for a plumber and they will flush the system until the water runs clear. Ensure that when they refill it they include a corrosion inhibitor to help prevent future problems.

Thermostatic valves are a great idea to have installed if you don't already have them – but this is really a job for a plumber, so I'm not going to explain how to do that here. However, what I will touch on is how to set them properly, as many people don't take advantage of them and therefore are paying more than necessary for their heating. Different rooms need different heating levels, and

a thermostatic valve allows you to set this at an individual room level. Recommended heating temperatures are 15°c for bedrooms, a slightly warmer 18°c for bathrooms and kitchens, and toasty 21°c for living rooms and dining rooms. That said, I often turn the thermostat right down in a dining room which isn't used often, or a spare bedroom, and just turn them up when I know they're going to be used.

Shower heads

An old shower head can often start to leak or become too clogged up with limescale to be able to properly clean it, or it may just be that you want to replace an old plastic white shower head and grubby hose with a smart new chrome one. This is a quick and easy job and doesn't involve any plumbing skills. Start by making sure that the water flow is diverted to the taps, as you would as if you wanted to run a bath. Then unscrew the base of the hose from the tap fittings and simply screw on the new hose. The shower head is attached in exactly the same way and merely screws into place.

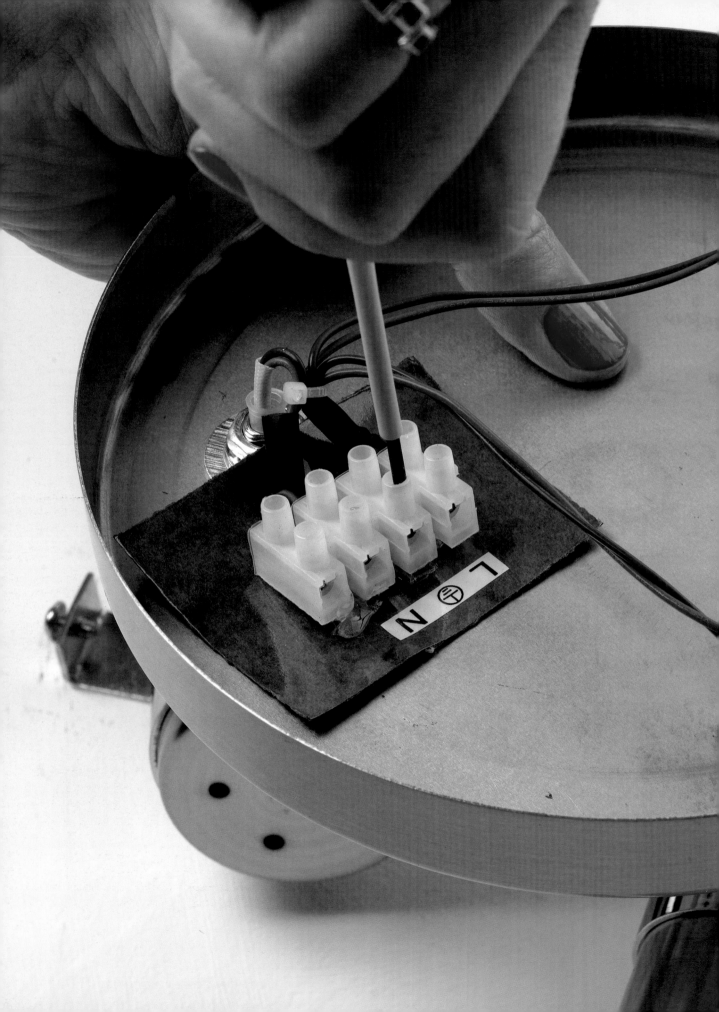

ELECTRICS

This is going to be a short chapter, because there are limited works that you are allowed to carry out yourself. At the time of writing, you are still allowed to change a plug, plug socket or light switch, and change a light fitting, as long as you are not working in a bathroom or kitchen. However, if you need anything moved or want anything new installed, or have any electrical work to be done in a 'wet' room (such as a bathroom or kitchen), or in the garden, you need to have this done and tested by a registered professional. It is highly advisable to check with your local authority's building control department first to see whether you need approval for what you are planning to do, or if it needs to be carried out by a certified professional.

ITEM:PLEXO 3LT SPOT ROUND
ITEM NO:30495
BARCODE:05240791
3XMax11W / GU10 CFL
SPECIALLY MADE IN CHINA FOR B&Q
240V~50Hz
B&QSO533YX/R10W18

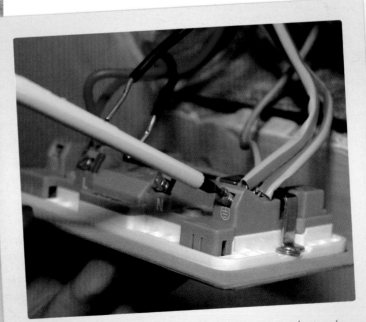

It's really not as scary as it looks.
Just follow the safety info

Read this first!

There are strict regulations about what you can and can't do yourself. If in doubt, always seek professional advice, and ensure you get a certificate for any works carried out. When carrying out work yourself, read this page first and make safety the number one priority.

Safety

When you're working on anything linked with the mains electricity, turn off the relevant switch in the mains unit – but if you are not sure which switch it is – then turn off the main switch.

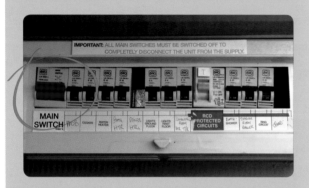

Also stick a large note on the consumer unit saying 'Do not switch on' as it just needs someone else in the house to wander in and think the electrics have tripped, casually flip the switch up and not realise that you are up a ladder changing a light fitting…

Tools for the job

There are only a few specialist items you need for electrical jobs.

* For obvious reasons, a light source that doesn't require electricity. Ideally a free standing torch that you can angle to the area where you are working, or a head torch – in both cases these will leave your hands free.
* A small stock of fuses, both plug fuses (3 amp and 13 amp) and also mains fuse cartridges if your consumer unit requires them.
* Electrical fittings use smaller than normal screws, so you will need screwdrivers with small heads – one flat head and one Phillips (cross head) will be sufficient.
* A pair of special electricians' pliers. Select a pair that has insulated handles, and in addition to jaws for shaping and cutting wires, a wire stripper function, so that you can cut through insulation without cutting through the wire.

Coloured wires

The colours used for wiring changed in 2004. Unless you're living in a new house or one that has been rewired since 2004, it's likely your sockets etc will have the old colours. Here is a table to show you what is, or was, what.

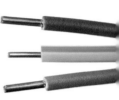

	Live	Neutral	Earth
Old colours	Red	Black	Green and yellow
New colours	Brown	Blue	Green and yellow

What's Watt

Watts are the measurement of power an electrical item uses. The table below shows you an average measurement for everyday items. If you want to cut down your bills, cut back on anything that generates heat (so hang that washing outside rather than using the tumbledrier).

Appliance	Watts
Electric Blanket	100
Clock	1
Dishwasher	3000
Fan heater	1000–3000
Food mixer	200
Fridge	100
Hair dryer	1500
Immersion heater	3000
Iron	500
Kettle	2000
Light bulb	7–150
Oven	3000–4000
Power drill	250
Radio	30
Towel rail	250
Tumble drier	2000
TV	350
Vacuum cleaner	250
Washing machine	3000

Fitting a plug

Many modern plugs are sealed units so you are not able to remove or change them without cutting the flex. However, if you have an appliance with an old style plug, here's a description of how to wire a new plug.

1 Start by unscrewing and removing the plug cover.

2 Then unscrew one side of the flex clamp whilst just loosening the other side.

3 Unscrew the three small wires from the pins.

4 Twist the metal strands at the end of the wires and place into the appropriate fixing hole in the new plug. Double check that they are all secured in place properly.

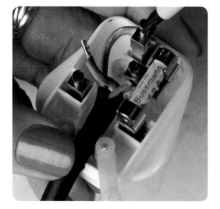

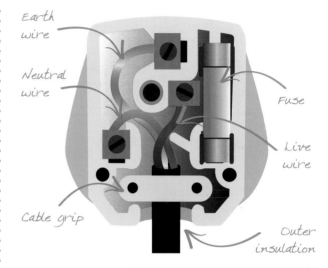

Earth wire

Neutral wire

Fuse

Live wire

Cable grip

Outer insulation

5 Make sure you are using the correct fuse for the appliance the plug is for.

6 Fasten the flex under the clamp and screw the plug cover back on.

If you are using a new piece of flex, you will need to carefully cut away the white or black outer cover using wire strippers, to about the length of the plug, making sure not to cut away the plastic coating on the three wires inside the flex.

Then cut each of the three wires to reach about 1cm past the appropriate screw. It's a good idea to make the earth wire as long as possible, so if the flex is pulled out accidentally, the earth is the last wire to disconnect. Using the strippers again, remove about 0.5cm of the three wires' plastic insulation.

Socket covers

Changing your socket covers is a neat way to set off a modern design in your room. Replacing the old white plastic ones with something funkier like chrome or brushed silver is one of the finishing touches, and you can tie them in with light switches and door handles.

The colour of the wires behind your sockets will depend on when the house was wired (see page 114)

1 Read the info on page 114. Unscrew the screw on each side of the socket and gently pull forward the front of the socket so that you can see and access the wiring behind it. The wires you see will be either from one, two or three cables, and accordingly there will be one, two or three wires of each colour.

2 The socket shown has two cables feeding it and hence two wires of each colour, red (live), black (neutral) and green with yellow stripes (earth). But the process is the same regardless of the number of each colour of cable.

Kerrie's top tip

Use your mobile phone or digital camera to take a photo of the wire positions before you remove them from the old cover, so you know what to put where in the new one.

Remember to use your insulated screwdriver for any electrical work

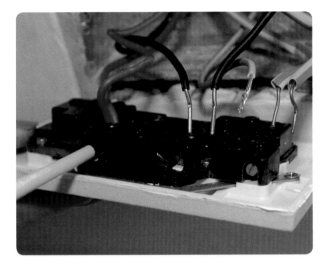

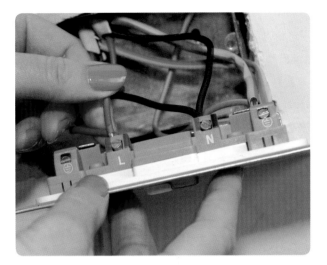

3 Unscrew the small terminal screws that hold the wires in place and remove the front of the old socket. You'll notice that the wires are quite stiff. Because this socket has a metal back box there are 3 earth wires – two on the ring main, the third to act as the earth to the back box (otherwise, the screws on a plastic cover, or the front of a metal cover would be live).

5 Wire up the new socket front by placing the red (or brown) into the live terminal, the black (or blue) into the neutral and the green with yellow stripes into the earth terminal. You need to make sure that the exposed metal part of each wire is inside the terminal and that none is visible outside the terminal.

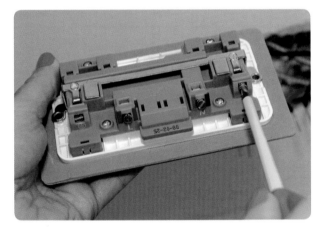

6 Then put the new socket front into place and, using a spirit level to make sure it's straight, screw it into place with the new screws provided. Metal sockets often come with a clear  plastic gasket (border) that you put against the wall before screwing the socket into place. This stops any damp from the plaster discolouring the metal.

4 Open up the terminals on the new socket to allow the wires to slot in, noting where the wires need to be positioned, then manipulate them gently to the right place. This is quite fiddly and you need to push them quite firmly.

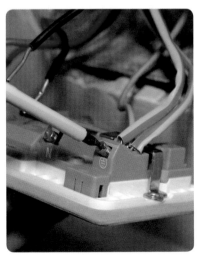

Light switches

In the same way as updating your socket covers, changing your light switches can add to the finish of a room. They may need changing purely because they have become discoloured, or cracked, so take the opportunity to replace them with something up to date that complements your décor.

Remember to use your insulated screwdriver for any electrical work

Our light switch had a metal back box, so we have shown you how to earth the new metal cover (in steps 3–6). If your switch doesn't have a metal back box, then you can skip this stage. If your fitting has more than one switch, the process will be similar, but I suggest making a note of how the old switch is wired before removing it, and replicating this on your new switch (a digital photo works well).

Kerrie's top tip

You can instantly change the mood in a room by switching off those bright main lights and using lamps. Candles add even more atmosphere (but make sure they're in a safe position).

1 Read the info on page 114. Make sure you have turned off the electricity at the consumer unit. Unscrew the two screws holding the plate in place and gently pull the plate forward so that you can see the wires.

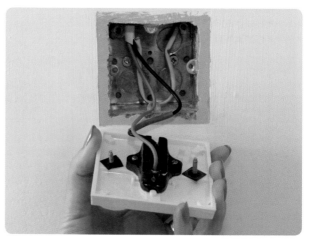

2 Unscrew the small terminal screws and remove the wires.

3 If you have a metal back box, you need to get hold of a length of earth wire and strip approximately 1cm off the end with wire strippers to expose the copper wire.

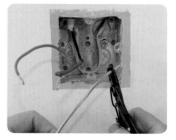

4 Then cut the earth wire to a length that will fit from the back box to the switch plate, again strip the end to expose the copper wire.

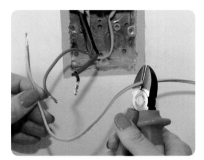

5 Fix one end of the earth wire to the earthing point on the back box.

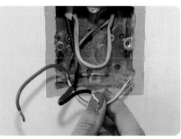

6 Then fix the other end to the earthing point on the switch plate (loosen the fixing screw first).

7 Line up the new front plate and carefully insert the bare end of the wires into the correct terminals and tighten the screws.

8 Put your new front plate in place and using a spirit level to ensure it's straight, screw it into place.

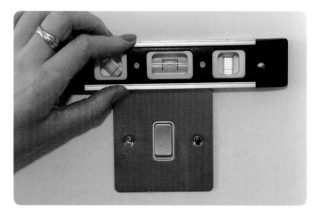

Light bulbs

Traditional light bulbs

✳ Traditional light bulbs are very inefficient at converting electricity to light, as they waste 95 per cent of the electricity they use in creating heat.

✳ 100 watt light bulbs were withdrawn from the shops in September 2009. By the end of 2011, 75 watt and 60 watt light bulbs will also be taken off the shelves. By 2012, all 40 watt and 25 watt bulbs will disappear from sale.

Energy saving light bulbs

✳ **Compact fluorescent lamps (CFLs):** these are the most common energy saving light bulbs and come in stick shape, candle shape, small or medium screw and bayonet fittings.

✳ **Energy saving halogen light bulbs:** a good option if you have halogen lights in your home. They consume around 30% less electricity than standard halogen bulbs.

✳ **LED lights:** these have progressed rapidly in recent years and can now be used to replace existing halogen spotlights.

Light fittings

This is an area that is often overlooked when we refurbish our home, but it is so important to the feel and usefulness of each room, and even the security of your home. Sketch out room plans and work out what lighting is needed where.

It is a good idea to start with the outside of the house, and the main concern here is security, so ideally have bright lighting at the front and back doors as this will also provide a welcome to your visitors.

The hallway should be warm but not over-bright, meanwhile making sure that there are no dark shadows on stairs; they should be clearly lit, not dangerously dark. In the kitchen you will need strong lighting, ideally fluorescent tubes or downlighters and under-cupboard lights. The latter are particularly useful as they won't cast a shadow over what you're doing.

For a dining room a central light is usually very suitable, ideally on a dimmer switch so it can be adjusted to suit the mood. But perhaps the most important room to get the lighting right in is the living room. The best way to achieve this is to have a variety of different sources of lighting. A main central light (or downlighters) is always useful – again a dimmer can be really handy here – and make sure the switch is by the door. Specific lighting for reading or watching TV, such as a standard lamp, can give a cosier feel, and you can also add effect lighting to highlight pictures, plants and so on.

Bedroom lighting is very much a matter of personal choice. If you like to read in bed, either have a bedside lamp, or an extra switch for the main light. If your partner doesn't like to read, make sure your side lamp has a narrow beam so they won't be disturbed.

Fitting a ceiling light

1 Read the info on page 114 and isolate the electricity by switching off the main switch on the consumer unit (or removing the fuse in an older unit). Unscrew the cover of the existing ceiling rose.

2 Make a note of the wires. In an older house you are likely to have red (live), black (neutral) and yellow/green (earth). In newer houses they'll be brown (live), blue (neutral) and yellow/green (earth). Our light is wired for a single switch so just has one set

of wires coming from the mains. In landings and large rooms where there's two switches operating the one light, you'll have double the amount of wires along with two switch wires.

3 Using a small insulated electrical screwdriver, remove the blue and brown wires (or red/black) from the terminal block. Then remove the earth wire.

4 Remove the screws holding the top of the ceiling rose in place.

5 Then squeeze the wires together and pull the fitting over them.

6 You're now left with the wires ready to install into your new light fitting.

7 Read the instructions carefully that come with your new light. Remove the fixing bracket from the back.

Bathroom lighting

Bathroom lights must be safe from water splashes and steam; a closed ceiling-mounted light is the normal choice. In addition, you may want an extra light above the mirror, so that you can ensure your make up is perfect! Either way, a switch inside the bathroom needs to be of the pull cord variety, whilst if it's outside the room it can be an ordinary switch.

8 Screw it in place next to the wires. You should find that most new fittings have the screw holes in the same position as the original ceiling rose. If not, you'll have to drill new ones and use suitable wallplugs (but check the ceiling for wires/pipes first).

9 Loosen the screws in the junction box on the light, noting which wire needs to go where.

10 Now find a friend and ask them to hold the light up close so you can put the wires into the junction box, making sure they are secured tightly in place.

11 Fix the fitting over the bracket and screw into place. (Then switch the mains back on and check everything works!)

Bright spark

By following the simple steps below, you can save yourself the stress, time and money when something goes wrong (and avoid that nightmare when the power goes off on the shower when you've still got shampoo in your hair).

Kerrie's top tip

Keep small torches in convenient places, upstairs and downstairs, so you always know where to find one if the power goes off in the dark.

It's dangerous to end up with an extension lead looking like this – get more twin sockets installed by a qualified electrician

Using a pro

Any electrician you use must be a NICEIC approved contractor. Don't feel embarrassed about asking for proof – your safety depends on it. Check out their credentials on the organisation's website www.niceic.org.uk. They also have a useful search function to help you find an approved contractor in your area. You are not allowed to do any electrical wiring work outside your home yourself, and there are also restrictions on what you can do inside.

Sensible precautions

There are a plenty of things you can do to make your home safer, and to keep yourself safe both when working with electricity and every day.

* Label the circuits in your consumer unit.
* Rewire if your home is old and it hasn't been done for a while (take the advice of a reputable electrician).
* Avoid overloading circuits. If your fuses keep blowing or switches keep tripping in your consumer unit, this is a warning sign that you should reduce the load on your ring circuit.
* Also avoid using multiplug extension cables. If you permanently need extra plugs, it is best to install a new twin socket onto the ring circuit.
* Check your appliances' flexes and plugs regularly for signs of wear and tear. Keep flexes away from sources of heat and never pull a plug out of a socket using the flex.
* Have your larger appliances regularly serviced.
* Water conducts electricity, so never mix the two. Don't stand vases of flowers on televisions; don't touch electrical items with wet hands and never use electrical appliances in the bathroom.
* Turn appliances off whenever possible, ideally by turning them off at the socket and unplugging them (this will also save you a lot of money rather than leaving them on standby).

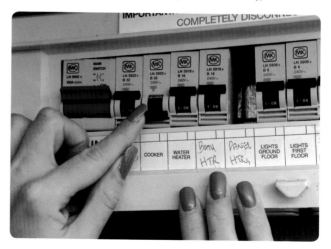

Troubleshooting

Light doesn't work

* Firstly check that other lights on the same circuit work. If so, the problem is isolated to one light. If not, see 'Circuit doesn't work'.
* First, turn off the light at the switch.
* Next, carefully remove the bulb (be careful; it may still be hot. If so, wrap a tea towel around your hand).
* If it is broken, you can remove the metal base by pushing a cork into the base, then press and twist.
* Install a new bulb and turn the switch on, facing away to protect your eyes just in case the new bulb breaks.
* If the light still doesn't work, then there is a problem with the rose itself.

Appliance doesn't work

* Firstly check that other appliances or pieces of equipment on the same circuit work, so that you can isolate the problem to just one appliance. If several are off, it's the circuit. See below.
* The most likely cause is that the fuse in the plug has blown. Switch the socket off and remove the plug. Check that the flex wires appear undamaged and remove the fuse.
* Check the fuse to see if it is blown (your multimeter should have this function) and assuming it is, replace it with a new fuse and refit the plug cover.
* If your appliance still doesn't work, then it is most likely a problem with the equipment itself and you should consult an electrician.

Circuit doesn't work

* If all the lights on one circuit don't work, or all the appliances on one circuit don't work, then the most likely reason is that the main fuse in the (older) consumer unit has blown or the circuit has tripped (in a newer consumer unit).
* This is most likely because the system is overloaded, but it could be that there is a fault with one of the outlet points.
* To isolate a faulty point, turn off each light or socket individually, repair the fuse or flip the trip switch, and then turn the lights or sockets on individually. If the fuse blows again, you have found the problem item, so follow the advice above.

Power in whole house doesn't work

* Firstly check the surrounding houses to see if it's a power cut. If it is a power cut, there is nothing you can do to repair it, but do go around the house unplugging everything other than the fridge and freezer (keep their doors closed to maintain their cold temperatures as long as possible) and turn off most of the lights.
* If the problem is isolated to your house, and you have a modern consumer unit, check that the main switch hasn't tripped. If it has, then reset it. In an older consumer unit check the fuses are all intact (see opposite for how to repair a fuse in the consumer unit).
* If the electricity does not come back on, or none of the fuses are blown, you need to contact your electricity provider immediately.

Blown fuse

Repairing a blown fuse in an old style consumer unit

* If the fuse blowing is due to overloading, then decrease the load on the circuit before repairing it by switching off or unplugging appliances, and ensure you don't overload it again.
* To replace the fuse, turn the main switch off, pull out the fuse carrier and remove the old fuse cartridge, and replace it with a new one.

* If you have a rewireable fuse, turn off the main switch, pull out the fuse carrier, then loosen the screws and remove all the old wire. Wind a length of new wire, the same length as the original piece, around one screw, and then pass enough wire through the fuse to allow you to wind it around the other terminal. Trim any excess wire before replacing the fuse carrier.

* It is then safe to turn the current back on. If the circuit is not overloaded, but the fuse keeps blowing, then you need to call an electrician.
* Never be tempted to put a higher fuse in place to stop it from blowing – fuses blow for a reason, and putting too high-rated a fuse in a circuit can cause a fire.

OTHER DIY JOBS

There's a lot of information in this book, but I'm never going to be able to cover absolutely every eventuality. So I did exhaustive research among my female friends, asking them about the sort of odd jobs they have around their homes and would like to be able to tackle themselves, and came up with a list of their top tasks. So here they are – the DIY greatest hits. We're going to start with how to put up various shelves, so you can display all your other half's football trophies (not!). You can then learn how to change the doors on your kitchen cupboards to give it a quick and inexpensive facelift, or just to repair or replace damaged hinges.

No more excuses. You can fix all those odd jobs yourself now

Shelving

There are lots of different shelves available on the market. Remember, you can choose a ready-made, freestanding unit (often flat packed) which means no drilling into walls is necessary.

Shelves are great for displaying your favourite ornaments

If you do choose a wall-mounted shelf, bear in mind how much weight you intend to place on it and also the construction of your wall ('floating' shelves and hollow walls can't take much weight). As always when drilling, check the area first using your wire and pipe detector to make sure that it is safe to drill into. I'm going to explain the two most popular options here, but the principles also apply to other shelving systems.

Kerrie's top tip

If you're using a lot of wall plug holes here's a good way to make it trouble-free. Using one screw in the first hole, screw it in fully and then remove it again. Continue for each wall plug hole until all have been fully bored by the screw. This helps when fixing an awkward or heavy shelf as it allows the weight to be taken quickly, easily and without straining yourself.

Floating shelves

These clever little inventions have the brackets hidden inside the chunky shelf itself so they appear to be floating on the wall. They are great for a couple of small, light ornaments, but anything heavier won't work. The shelf ought to come with instructions, which you should follow carefully, but here are the basics.

1 There are normally two wall brackets. Hold the first in place and mark through the fixing holes where you need to drill.

2 Drill your hole (using the appropriate drill bit), put the appropriate wall plugs in (hollow or solid wall), and then loosely screw the bracket in place.

3 Then use the shelf to help position the second bracket. Hold the bracket on the wall and slide the shelf onto both brackets (there will be two circular holes in the back of the chunky shelf). Using your spirit level ensure the shelf is straight, and when it is, mark the position of the second bracket.

4 When the second bracket is in place, double check that it's level and then slot the shelf into position and tighten the retaining screws under the shelf to hold it in place on the brackets.

Adjustable shelves

These are a great invention as you can change the height of the shelves to suit your purposes – and if you decide at a later stage to put tall books in a different place, you can just move the brackets and shelf to suit.

1 Make sure the supports will be about 10cm in from the end of the shelf. Hold the support against the wall and mark the top fixing point through the hole.

2 Drill the hole (once you've checked for wires and pipes), push the correct wall plugs into the holes, and screw the support into place.

Push the support to the side to drill the other holes

3 Use a spirit level to check the support is straight and continue to mark the remaining holes. Push the support to the side and drill and plug the holes.

4 Now get the next vertical support and hold it in place, using your spirit level across the top to ensure they line up – be careful which way up the support is, as sometimes they are different from top to bottom. Make sure the second one is the same way around as the first. Repeat the same procedure as above for fixing the support in place.

5 Put the brackets into the supports at the height you want them, starting with the top shelf. Make sure both brackets are the same number of slots down from the top so that the shelf will be level.

6 Place the wooden shelf into place on the brackets and check the overhang is equal either end. Use your bradawl to make pilot holes on the bottom of the shelf through the supports. Again, start with the top, as there's then space to work.

7 Remove the shelf and drill small pilot holes, being careful not to drill right through the shelf (put some tape around the drill bit to mark the correct depth to be on the safe side). Put the shelf back into position and screw it to the brackets.

Changing kitchen doors

This is an easy way to transform the look of your kitchen without going to the expense of installing new cupboards. It is also a useful skill if you have one problematic door that needs adjusting or replacing. In addition to your normal tools, you will need a hinge cutting bit to attach to your drill.

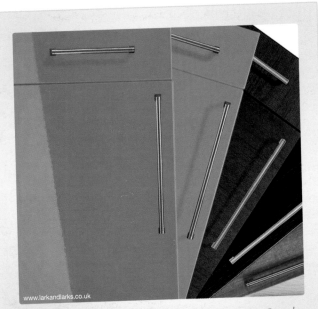

www.larkandlarks.co.uk

New modern kitchen doors and a fresh colour paint on the walls will give your kitchen an economical makeover

Kerrie's top tip

If you don't want to replace all of the doors in your kitchen, a cheap and fast way to freshen them up is to paint them. Make sure you buy a primer made for the material your doors are made from, though, to ensure a good and long lasting finish.

1 Firstly, remove the door by loosening the rearmost retaining screw and sliding the hinge out of the hinge plate.

Hinge

Hinge plate

2 Then unscrew the hinge from the inside of the old door.

3 Most replacement doors come with a hinge recess in place, but if not, use a hinge cutting bit to drill out the recess into the door, but be careful not to go too deep. Make sure you've measured the correct position on the door so that the hinge will then slot into the existing hinge plates inside the cupboard.

Hinge hole cutter

4 Push the hinge into its new position and check that it's straight. Mark the position of the holes and drill pilot holes. Then fix the screws in place. If the old hinge plate screws have become loose it's good practice to put the hinge in a new position to ensure solid fixings.

5 Rehang the door. If you find the door hinge doesn't match up with the hinge plates inside the cupboard, then you'll need to reposition the hinge plates by unscrewing, marking new positions, drilling pilot holes and rescrewing. You can cover up any holes with filler.

Misaligned doors

To adjust a door that is misaligned, there are adjusting screws on kitchen door hinges. Simply tighten or loosen the relevant screw to lift or drop the door, or move it slightly left or right. Try not to let the screws come completely out, as the door may come loose, but otherwise just adjust one, test to see what effect it's had, then try again until it's straight and closes neatly.

Height Adjustment

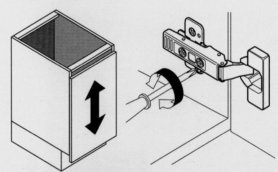

Depth Adjustment

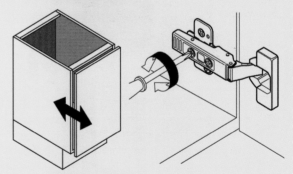

Side Adjustment

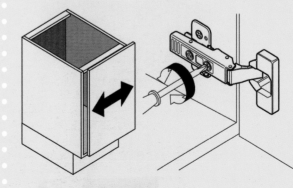

Hanging a picture

There are lots of nail and hook combinations which just need to be hammered into the wall and are quick and easy to use. However, for a mirror, a picture with glass, or anything that's slightly heavier, I would always recommend using a screw and wall plug combination for greater security.

Satisfaction. There's no need to wait for someone else to put up your pics now

For larger frames and mirrors always use screws and wall plugs

1 Firstly find someone to help (if you can drag him away from the football/rugby/women's gymnastics) and get them to hold the picture in the correct position. When you're happy, put your spirit level on top to make sure it's straight and gently mark the top corners with little L shapes, in pencil. You can now allow your other half to get back to the telly.

2 Now measure and mark the midway point between the two marks – this will be the centre of the top of the frame when it's hanging, but more importantly this is the vertical line on which you want your fixing.

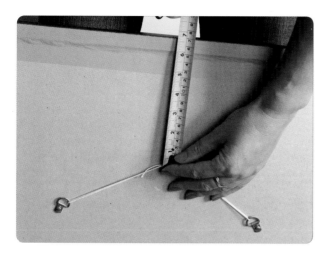

3 Now grab your picture and use the end of your tape measure to pull the string or wire up as if it were hanging, and then measure the distance to the top of the frame.

This dictates how much below the top of the frame you need to secure your fixing to the wall, so measure down from the central mark you made earlier and make another mark.

Multiple pictures

When hanging multiple pictures together, consider the final effect before marking and drilling. It is an idea to lay them out on a clear space on the floor and play around with which you want where, the distances between them, and the heights you want them at. With two pictures you can hang them exactly side-by-side, one under the other, or at angles to each other, for example. Experiment to see what looks best and what suits the style of pictures – whether portrait, landscape or a mixture. Equally you can create some great effects with three or many more pictures, but do a plan on the floor before you start measuring, marking and drilling the wall.

Check for hidden pipes and wires before drilling

5 Screw the fixing into place – remembering not to screw it in all the way so that your picture's wire has something to hang on.

If you are screwing into a hollow wall, and you are right over a wooden joist (ideal) then you can screw straight into that. Otherwise you'll need a special hollow wall plug.

6 Now you are ready to hang the picture and have a final check with your spirit level to make sure it's straight and adjust as necessary.

4 After checking for pipes and wires using your detector, use a suitable drill bit and drill your hole, pop in a suitable wall plug for your type of wall and the weight of the picture or mirror you are hanging.

Kerrie's top tip

By this point you'll have several marks on the wall, so when marking the position you need to drill, put a little tick next to the mark so that once you come back with your drill you're in no doubt as to which mark you're working from.

Resealing bath and basin edges

Over time, even 'mould proof' silicone can discolour and become mouldy, making your bathroom look dirty and unloved. If the silicone has shrunk, moved or split, it may also mean that water leaks through on to the floor when you have a shower, which is altogether more serious.

A soak in the bath can be the perfect place to unwind, so spend a bit of time tidying up your bathroom

If you like picking at things, then you'll enjoy this bit! Remove any loose strips of silicone first.

1 Remove the remaining silicone completely, using a Stanley knife blade to gently cut it away from the tiles and the top of the bath/basin. Be careful not to damage the surface of your bath.

You can buy a special silicone remover tool that makes it an easier job. For a really tidy result, you can then paint on some silicone remover fluid. Leave this for 15 minutes and then wipe it off.

2 Clean and dry the area ready for the new silicone, but before you begin – trust me on this – strip off and run yourself a nice warm bath! (There is no need to do this for a basin, although filling it with water is advisable.) Whilst I am an advocate of well deserved relaxation, naked DIY isn't necessarily advisable – however, the method behind this madness is that a full bath (water plus a person) is a lot heavier than an empty bath, and therefore it will sit slightly lower. If you silicone it when it's in this position it will remain sealed when full. However, if you silicone it when it's empty, then once it's full of water and you, the weight and subsequent movement can break the silicone away from the bath meaning you don't have a water-tight finish. Before you get in, have to hand your silicone gun and a packet of wet wipes.

3 Gently gun a neat bead of silicone all along the ends and edge of the bath, at the joining point of the bath and tiles.

4 Now use your finger and gently smooth the bead of silicone so that it forms a convex shape between the tiles and the bath edge – and use the baby wipes to remove the excess silicone from your finger each time.

There are many old husbands' tales about the best way to do this and you can buy various contraptions to do it (or smother your finger in washing up liquid first) but I find baby wipes and a finger by far the best option.

Now why not relax and enjoy the bath as you're already in it – but be careful not to get the silicone wet when you get out. Leave the water in the bath until the silicone has set (see the tube for details of how long this takes as it can vary).

Relax and enjoy the fruits of your labour

Changing a toilet seat

This is a simple task, and a new loo seat can really help to update a room quickly. But there are a few simple rules to follow to prevent that awful feeling of sitting down, the seat slipping and you feeling like you're going to fall off!

1 First remove the old seat. Use a screwdriver to lift off any caps and remove the screws.

2 Your new seat will have adjustable hinges so they can be moved into the right position to fit the holes in your pan. Follow the instructions to adjust these into the correct position to fit your pan and secure them firmly using the screws provided.

3 Fit the long bolts into place and put the large seat washers over the top on to the hinge plate – be careful not to drop anything down the loo (putting cling film over the pan is a good idea, but remember to take it off!)

4 Hold the seat and lid upright, and slide the two long fixing bolts through the holes in your pan, ensuring the hinge plates sit flush onto the top of the pan (adjust if necessary).

You will be able to see the end of the bolts below the pan rim, at the back. From underneath at the back, slide the plastic domed washers onto the fixing bolts and then screw on the nuts.

5 Tighten them finger tight, but be careful not to overtighten them. Then show him how easy it is to put the seat down – especially when it's fitted with a 'soft close' action!

Skirting boards

Skirting boards can drastically alter the look of a room, and are a great way to modernise your house by replacing old ones with something less fiddly and intricate. They are also functional in that they protect the base of the wall from furniture – and over-zealous vacuuming!

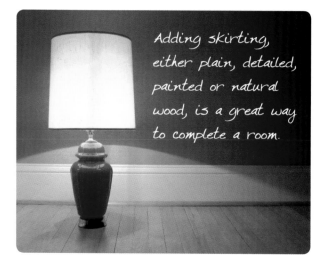

Adding skirting, either plain, detailed, painted or natural wood, is a great way to complete a room.

There is a special piece of kit you will need for this job, and that is a mitre block. This clever gadget helps you to cut things like skirting boards, dado rails and coving at angles so that the corners fit together. It has different angles already laid out to guide your saw, depending on whether you're cutting an internal corner, an external corner or another angle. Read the instructions carefully and, if in doubt, practise on a couple of old offcuts of wood before laying into your new skirting.

The other thing which is really handy is some grab adhesive, such as No More Nails which comes either in a tube that you can squeeze, or better still in a cartridge that you can put into a gun like the professionals. It is easier to apply this way, too.

Two things to check before you start, as with any drilling or nailing job, are that you know and avoid the location of any wires and pipes (using your detector) and secondly that you know the construction of your walls so that you can select the correct wall plugs.

Mitre block

1 Measure and cut your lengths of skirting accordingly. If you are joining to a door frame or architrave, then you will need to cut the end of the skirting board straight. However, if you are going into an internal corner, or an external corner, you will need to use your mitre block to achieve the correct angle on the two adjoining pieces of skirting.

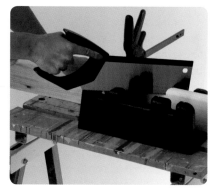

2 Before securing the two pieces of skirting at an internal corner, push them both into place to make sure that you've cut the angle correctly and adjust if necessary. They should fit tightly together.

3 Next, glue the boards into place using your adhesive – the best way is to draw a wiggly line on the back of each board, but not too near the edges so it won't spill out when pushed into place.

4 The next step depends on your wall type. If you have stud walls, you can very easily just use nails ('lost-head' nails are ideal) to nail the board into place, onto each stud. Two nails per stud are sufficient.

5 If you have solid or masonry walls, then you may be able to use masonry nails, but if you can't get these to go into the wall (some walls are just too solid) then you will need to first drill a hole through the skirting into the wall and then push a wall plug into the hole by hand, tapping it flush with a hammer.

6 Hang on to the hammer, as now you need to put a screw into the wall plug and knock that in gently until you feel firm resistance (ie when it reaches the wall), and then tighten it right up using your screwdriver. The screw needs to be long enough to go through the skirting board and into the wall. As with nailing, fix another screw below the first, and repeat every 50cm or so.

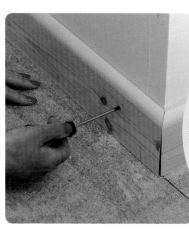

7 The only difference when fixing an external corner is that you need to glue the corners themselves together. Drill small pilot holes as guides (and also to stop the wood splitting) and nail in lost head nails at the corner; two should be fine. Use a nail punch to sink the nail head into the wood.

Kerrie's top tip
The reason you should use lost head nails and countersunk screws is so that you can easily fill, sand and paint them afterwards to cover up any sign of the fixings. If you don't do this, you can be left with ugly screw heads showing on your finished skirting.

Fitting coving

Coving is not dissimilar to skirting in how it is fitted – but the added complication is that you are working at ceiling level so it's a little harder to do it on your own. If you can persuade someone to hold the other end whilst you're working, life will be a lot easier.

From plain to decorative – coving can help to 'frame' a room and adds contrast when using stong colours on the walls

In terms of extra tools, you will need a mitre block, plus coving adhesive suitable for the type of coving you have bought.

Cornices and Roses

If you live in an older house you may have original decorative cornices and ceiling roses. Minor repairs using plaster of Paris are possible, but if you need to replace a large area, specialist firms can make moulds from your existing patterns.

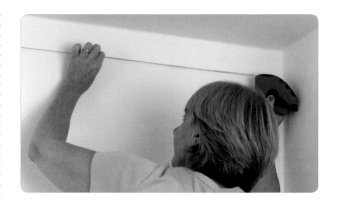

1 The pack of coving will give you a measurement of the distance down from the ceiling the coving will sit. Measure this out and draw a pencil line all around the room, or use a chalk line.

2 Also note on the back of the coving it may say which is the top or ceiling edge of the coving. It's often just marked along the top edge. This is important when you come to cut corners.

3 For long straight areas, simply apply adhesive to the coving's top and bottom (there is no point in gluing the middle, as this doesn't touch the wall or ceiling).

4 Press the coving into place, positioning it up against the chalk or pencil lines (this is where a helper is useful), and wipe away any excess adhesive with a sponge.

5 Then gently nail in a few nails underneath the coving (having checked the area for pipes and cables with your detector first) so that the nails help to take the weight of the coving while the adhesive is drying.

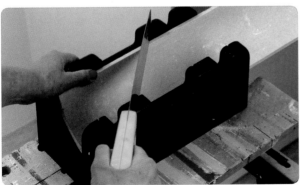

6 Corners should be cut using a mitre block; angles will differ for internal and external corners, and depending on whether you're fitting a left-hand piece or a right-hand piece. Make sure you put the coving the right way up into the mitre block. If in doubt, practise on a small offcuts first.

External mitre

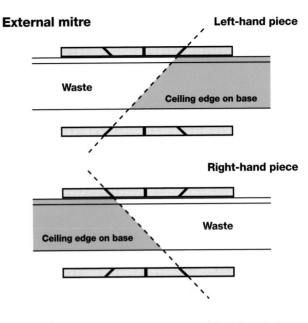

Left-hand piece

Waste

Ceiling edge on base

Right-hand piece

Ceiling edge on base

Waste

Internal mitre

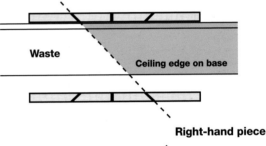

Left-hand piece

Waste

Ceiling edge on base

Right-hand piece

Ceiling edge on base

Waste

7 Line the cut pieces up first to ensure a good fit before applying adhesive.

There is a greater margin for error with coving as you can apply caulk to any gaps before decorating to hide any slight imperfections in your angles – but I'm sure you won't need to do that...

Wall tiling

Replacing the old fashioned tiles in your bathroom or kitchen can transform the room in a relatively short period of time. Often if a whole bathroom is looking tired, changing the tiles alone is enough to perk it up and save you investing in a whole new bathroom suite.

Once you've tried your hand at a small area of tiling, you could then plan a whole room

Check the measurement of your tile and work out how many tiles you'll need to fill the space. If you end up with a small width of tile to fit an edge space, it's worth adjusting your starting point to off-centre, so you then have more than half a tile width to fill an edge.

Kerrie's top tip

Coloured tiles may vary in shade from batch to batch. Using tiles from one box at a time may result in colour changes across the surface. However, variations in shade will be far less noticeable if you mix tiles from different boxes before you begin work.

1 Once you have fixed your starting point with battens, spread tile adhesive over an area not more than 1sq m.

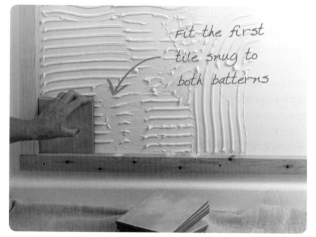

Fit the first tile snug to both battens

2 Place the first tile in position so that it sits on the horizontal batten and is hard up against the vertical batten. Press it firmly into the adhesive.

3 Add the next horizontal tile and the first tile of the row above.

4 Continue to add tiles over the area with adhesive, using tile spacers as you go. When that area is complete, wipe over it with a cloth or sponge as it's essential to remove any adhesive on the surface of the tiles before it hardens. Continue working in this way until the main area requiring tiles is completed.

5 When you reach a corner or edge that requires a cut tile, measure the top and bottom of the gap. Mark the measurements on the tile with a felt pen (remembering that the cut edge is the one that goes into the corner).

6 Cut it with a tile cutter (see page 77 for using a manual cutter).

7 Then file any rough edges, holding the file at right angles to the edge.

8 Place the cut piece of tile in the gap to check it fits correctly.

9 Spread a layer of adhesive on the back of the tile and put firmly in place.

10 When tiling is complete and the adhesive has dried (check the manufacturer's instructions as drying times vary), spread grouting across the tiles and into the joints.

11 Then immediately wipe over the tiles with a damp sponge to remove any grout from the face of the tiles, but taking care not to dig any out from the joints.

12 Allow the grout to harden slightly then you can shape the joints, removing any surplus grout with a sponge or grout shaper.

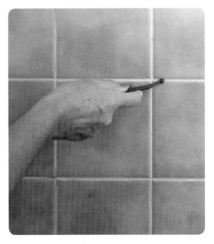

Replacing tiles

You will need your tiling equipment for this job plus a grout scraper to rake out grout (available at all DIY stores) and a brick bolster or old chisel to help chip out the offending tile.

Hang on to those old spare tiles as accidents can happen

1 Sheet up the area you are working in very well, so that you protect your bath surface, sink or floor from sharp pieces of falling tile. Put on some eye protection. Start by using your grout scraper to scrape away as much of the old grout as possible around the cracked tile you wish to remove. Lean towards the cracked tile, so that if you slip or chip an edge it's the damaged tile anyway.

2 Next, using a suitable bit, drill numerous random holes into the tile that you're removing – this will help to loosen it and make it easier to remove. You'll need to push quite hard against the tile.

3 Now you can use the bolster or chisel to loosen and remove sections of the tile, but make sure you have your gloves on when you start handling the pieces of tile.

Kerrie's top tip

A ceramic tile drill bit is designed to bite immediately into the glaze of a tile without skidding, removing the need for masking tape or breaking through the glaze with a sharp pointed tool. Various sizes of bit are available to suit a range of hole diameters.

Replacing a broken tile is not quite as easy as tiling from scratch, because you have to be very careful not to damage the surrounding tiles in the process of removing the broken one.

Tile cutting drill bits

4 You now need to prepare the surface to receive the new tile, so start by removing as much of the old adhesive as possible with a scraper. If you don't do this, your new tile will sit proud of the old tiles.

5 Now you can fit your new tile in place using fresh adhesive, and use tile spacers to make sure that the tile is aligned perfectly with the surrounding tiles.

6 When the adhesive is dry remove the spacers, and then grout and clean around the tile.

Regrouting

Regrouting can transform the look of a tired bathroom or kitchen fairly easily, and certainly very cheaply. All you need to do is rake out the old grout along every joint of every tile (yes it is just as much hard work as it sounds and you may regret it once you've started, but persevere as the end results will make it worthwhile).

Be very careful not to damage any of the edges of the tiles in the process. Then simply clean away all the dust (a vacuum cleaner is particularly effective) and apply grout, as described in the tiling chapter. Clean off the excess with a damp sponge, and finish it off by using your finger, or a grout shaper down the joints. Give the tiles a final clean and polish once the grout is dry.

Kerrie's top tip

For a real cheat, and to save the need to regrout, if you have white grout you can buy a grout pen from DIY stores and you literally draw over the existing grout. It's not as effective as regrouting, but it will perk up your room in about a tenth of the time.

SOLVING PROBLEMS

In previous chapters I've not only described how to refurbish and refit parts of your home, but also how to deal with problems that can affect its fixtures and fittings. But there are also lots of things that can, and will, go wrong with your home itself, so in this chapter I'll explain how to deal with and prevent some of the more common issues. Problem partners not included, I'm afraid… The issues we are going to deal with here include condensation, mould and damp, subsidence and wood decay, unwelcome visitors (and I don't mean the 'in-laws/out-laws'), heat loss and fire prevention.

Follow my partner's life-saving advice on pages 152–153

Problems

The problems that we are looking at are the most common issues that affect many homes. As well as learning how to deal with them, we're going to look at how to prevent them from occurring in the first place.

Condensation

Amazingly, an average family produces 20 litres of moisture in the home every day, mainly from cooking, washing and showers or baths, but also around one litre each from breathing and perspiring. If your man is particularly sweaty this could be even higher (you can blame him rather than your one-and-a-half-hour bubble bath)!

We've done such a good job of insulating our homes against drafts and heat loss that an unfortunate by-product is an increase in water vapour trapped inside the home, and therefore condensation.

Warm air, especially in a kitchen or bathroom, has a particularly high water content. When this air meets a cold surface such as a tile or window, condensation in the form of water droplets appears. Most of this time this is easily dealt with by wiping the surface, but it can lead to problems if the water starts to drip on to wooden or metal surfaces, which can rot or rust.

Prevention of excessive condensation is really easy – simply ventilate your home well; especially the rooms with specific problems. Ideally, close the bathroom or kitchen door and open the window, and ventilate other rooms regularly too to allow a change of air. If your home is well ventilated but you still have condensation problems, it may be that there isn't enough heat, so try and leave a small amount of dry heat on during the day (for instance the central heating on low) rather than just for a few hours in the morning and evening – but avoid paraffin heaters as they'll just create more condensation.

Use extractor fans where you have them in kitchens and bathrooms, and make sure your tumble drier vents to the outside.

Mould

Mould is not only unsightly, but can actually be bad for your health – the airborne spores of some types of mould can pose a health hazard by causing breathing problems. If you have mould in the home, it is an indication that the environment is not right, so don't ignore it – either there is insufficient ventilation and/or there is damp coming in through the walls or roof.

Mould is most likely to occur in bathrooms and kitchens, and on painted wooden surfaces, but can also spring up in dark corners – inside wardrobes and so on – in particularly poorly ventilated homes. It can even form on fabrics and clothing, when it's technically then called mildew.

Dealing with mould is relatively simple:
* Wipe down the affected area with a diluted bleach solution.
* The following day, scrape off any remaining mould.
* If you have mouldy wallpaper, remove it and burn it.
* Make sure you use a fungicidal wallpaper paste and sealer when redecorating.
* Prevention of mould falls under the same diagnosis as condensation and damp, so refer to those sections for further guidance.

Damp

There are various types of damp that can affect your home, and all should be taken seriously, and resolved before you tackle cosmetic remedies such as blocking stains and repainting walls. The decorating chapter explains how to make the walls look good again, but make sure you, or a professional, tackle the cause first.

✳ **Traumatic damp** is water from an inside source, such as a leaky pipe or drain, reaching the wall or ceiling. A tell-tale sign is that the size of the patch gradually increases.

✳ **Penetrating damp** is caused by outside water, from rain or snow, finding its way inside to walls or ceilings. This is typically found around window frames and is more likely on north and west facing walls. If the mark is long and thin, it's most likely from a leaky guttering down pipe. These patches will increase in size after rain, and decrease during a dry period.

✳ **Rising damp** is when water from the ground reaches the floor or wall. This is actually fairly uncommon, but can manifest itself by a damp patch on a wall, or lifting wallpaper or even floor tiles.

'First aid for the home' kit

I described at the beginning of this book what you need in your toolkit, but one of the most important kits you can get together is actually a house-saving kit – namely all the bits and pieces that you might need to avoid or deal with an emergency.

Your house-saving kit should contain items such as waterproof tape for tackling leaking pipes, a selection of fuses, a fire blanket and fire extinguisher, and some form of emergency lighting and heating in the case of a power failure. In addition, include a list of useful numbers such as electrician, police station, doctor, 24-hour plumbing service and emergency gas service. Keep it somewhere easily accessible in a hurry, ideally in a similar place to your first aid kit, and if the worst happens you'll be well prepared.

Fire blanket
Read the instructions as soon as you buy it.

Fire extinguisger
Buy one that's suitable for all types of fire.

Waterproof tape
For leaking pipes.

First aid kit
For you and your family.

Torch
In case the lights go out.

Subsidence

There are many causes of subsidence, most are unavoidable but I'll explain them so you understand why it happens before I explain how to spot it and what to do about it.

Subsidence is basically a downward movement of the home, which causes structural damage. Upward movement can also occur, which is called heave.

Subsidence can be caused by the subsoil moving, through swelling and shrinking during particularly wet winters or dry summers for example, which puts great strain on the building's foundations. The subsoil's stability can also be affected by many other factors, such as floods, old mining works, underground rivers, uptake of water by tree roots, insufficient settlement time prior to building and so on. Rarely, but not unheard of, subsidence can be caused by the foundations themselves not having been properly laid.

One factor within your control (though this isn't always the case) is not planting trees too close to the home. Large trees should be at least 15m away, small trees 5m – but also bear in mind you may not be allowed to remove a tree if it has a protection order on it, and that you can sometimes make a problem worse by removing a tree, as the water content in a clay subsoil will change quickly and can lead to heave.

Symptoms that could indicate your property is suffering from subsidence include doors and windows sticking and cracks in the walls. If you suspect you have subsidence don't delay; call an expert immediately.

Most cracks are harmless – small, drying-out cracks for example. Less than 3mm wide is not a cause for concern, but if they're larger than that make sure you examine them more carefully. Long cracks are more worrying than short ones, and cracks in the corners of a house, or running diagonally from a window or door can mean subsidence. A common place to spot a subsidence crack is where an extension or garage joins the main home, which could well indicate a problem with the foundations of the added-on building.

If you are in any doubt, or if you think you do have subsidence, call in a surveyor. Unfortunately, remedial works are expensive and disruptive and may involve underpinning foundations, inserting steel ties, or even rebuilding the affected area. However, you may be covered on your home insurance, so always check this first.

Wood decay

There is no cure for wood decay – commonly known as dry rot or wet rot – so prevention here is vital.

Wood decay is caused by airborne spores infecting the wood, and then wood-rotting strands spreading outwards. This can only occur if the wood is damp or wet, and has been for some time, so it's really important to protect your home against damp, and to use preservative treatment in high-risk areas.

Dry rot

Dry rot begins in a damp, poorly ventilated place – most commonly suspended wooden floors, cellar timbers, leak-affected structural timber and the back of skirting boards. It prefers damp rather than wet timber.

The wood-rotting strands are strong enough to penetrate plaster, mortar and even brick, so this is a particularly serious type of rot.

It is hard to spot as it's usually hidden from sight, but you may notice a mushroomy smell, and the wood will be soft if you poke it with a screwdriver. The spores look like red dust and you may spot woolly growths above skirting boards.

This is definitely a job for a professional (and ask for a guarantee) as all infected wood needs to be cut back at least one metre from the affected area, and all strands removed from plaster, brickwork etc. Special fungicide should also be applied to all other wood, and the source of damp should be found and addressed.

wisepropertycare.com

Wet rot

Wet rot attacks wet, rather than moist timber. It will not spread to moist timber and can only survive in wet timber, so it is often found outside the home, and in localised areas such as window sills, door frames and fence posts. The symptoms are fairly obvious in that the paint will bubble, the wood below will be soft and dark in colour, and it will crack along the grain of the wood. Prevention inside is by way of good ventilation and allowing wood to dry thoroughly following a leak. Outside, ensure wood is thoroughly and regularly protected with paint or a stain/preservative. Dealing with wet rot is reasonably straightforward. Cut away the rotten timber and replace it with preservative-treated wood. For smaller areas you can use a special wood filler, once you have removed the rotten parts and painted the edges of the remaining wood with hardener.

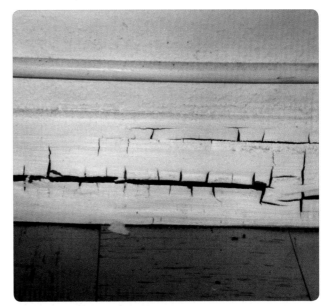

Infestation

Pests come in many forms, not all of which are harmful but may be disturbing. Some are microscopic and others are all too visible (no, I'm not going to opt for the obvious man gag here).

Ants

Spray with an ant aerosol; trace back to the nest if possible, and pour boiling water on it. Put a puff of ant powder at the nest entrance.

Bats

They're harmless, and protected by law. Contact your local council who will arrange for their removal for you. It's illegal to try this yourself.

Bed bugs

These are round, 3mm bugs that feed on human blood and can causing irritating little bites and a strange smell. They are fairly uncommon, though currently on the increase, and can be present in old mattresses for example. They can be killed by insecticidal sprays, but this is best left to a professional.

Carpet beetles

These little chaps attack carpets, woollens, fur etc. They are about 3mm long and you can spot their presence by their little cast-off furry skins. They love to live in bird nests, so remove any you may have in your loft, and make sure you have no fluff around in wardrobes and drawers. Spray your carpet with carpet beetle killer.

Clothes moths

These are pale and about 8mm long, and actually don't do any harm, but their grubs do! The grubs eat woollen blankets, clothes, carpets, and fur and are attracted by perspiration and food residues. Moth repellants work well, as does storing blankets in plastic bags, and there are also moth aerosols on the market.

Cockroaches

The picture reminds me of my university hall of residence, which was infested with these horrible little critters, scuttling about in the dining room every night after dark. It is thought that they can cause food poisoning, and they certainly leave an unpleasant smell. Spray nooks and crannies in kitchens with a suitable aerosol, and repeat as necessary.

Fleas

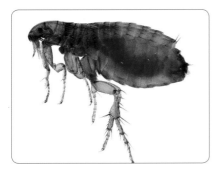

The tell-tale sign of fleas is small red bites that are very itchy. The fleas are likely to have come from your pet, so make sure you give them regular flea treatment and in the meantime burn old, infested bedding and vacuum your carpets and furniture thoroughly. You can also buy aerosols and sprays to treat your carpets and furniture.

Mice

These speedy little chaps can fit through the tiniest of holes in a wall or cupboard, leaving telltale small droppings, and will nibble on food, packages and, perhaps most worryingly, electrical cables. They can also carry food poisoning, so it's important to deal with them quickly. Use mouse bait, ensure any entry points are blocked, and if necessary, resort to traps.

Mites

These are absolutely tiny and only just visible to the naked eye – they look like moving particles of dust. Dust mites live on particles of dead skin, and furniture mites live in upholstery. Some people are allergic to one or both types so if you are wheezing try plastic-filled pillows and vacuum your bedroom daily.

Rats

These intruders are truly revolting, and pretty scary at around 20cm long. Apparently in London you are never further than one metre from a rat – not a comforting thought, and a good advert for living in the countryside in my view! Rats can damage pipes and cables, and carry numerous diseases, so contact your council immediately.

Silverfish

These are weird little creatures who thrive in damp areas and can munch on wallpaper paste (I said they were weird!). They don't cause a problem in themselves but they can indicate a damp problem. You're most likely to spot them in sinks and baths. They can be killed with an aerosol if you don't like seeing them around.

Spiders

In the UK these are fortunately totally harmless (not so in other countries, so be grateful!). A web outside may indicate an area of dampness, whilst indoors it just shows a lack of regular dusting (harsh but fair). There are spider catchers on the market that help you to catch and release them into the wild outside if you're too squeamish to lift them up.

Precautions

As a general rule, maintaining good hygiene is an obvious precaution – don't allow old food scraps or crumbs to lie around anywhere, don't have compost heaps too close to the home, and fill gaps along skirting boards and around pipes where they enter from outside.

Cures come in many forms too. It's worth keeping a safe multi-use aerosol to hand (but read the label carefully before using). Don't spray around food, children or animals. Serious infestations – wasps, rats and so on – will require professional help.

Heat loss

These is no such thing as a heat-proof home – and neither should there be, since ventilation is essential. However, you can reduce your fuel bills and also the environmental impact of your home by taking some basic steps.

Roof
Roofs lose around a quarter of your heat – easily tackled via loft insulation, opposite. If the loft is used, or planned to be used as a habitable space, then special roof lining will be required rather than loft insulation. This is best left to professionals, since ventilation considerations are important.

Walls
Walls are worth attention as almost half the heat lost is via this route. If you have cavity walls they can be foam-filled to provide insulation; if the walls are solid, you can install insulated plasterboard on the inside.

This thermal image shows the benefits of cavity wall insulation used in the yellow house.

www.ashdenawards.org

Doors and windows
Doors and windows are responsible for about a quarter of heat lost – mainly through cracks and gaps. It is always worthwhile draughtproofing doors and windows (as discussed in an earlier chapter), however, replacing glass is not always economical as comparatively little heat is lost through the glass itself and it is an expensive job to install double glazing.

Ground floor
About an eighth of all heat lost is through the floors of the ground floor. Insulation can be installed below wooden floors on the ground floor to reduce this. Thick carpet underlay is also effective, and make sure any holes and gaps between the floor and skirting are filled.

Loft insulation

Loft insulation is always worthwhile and reduces heat loss significantly, so that's what I'm going to concentrate on explaining here.

Before you start, make sure that you have a safe working platform to stand on – never step between joists, and make sure you are wearing protective goggles, a dust mask and gloves. Overalls are a good idea to stop dust and fibres from getting lodged in your clothes.

Current recommendations are for 30cm of loft insulation – so check the depth of the rolls that you are buying and calculate the quantity you need accordingly. A 15cm roll will require two layers, for example.

1 Before laying the insulation, put a layer of plastic membrane down to help prevent condensation problems in the loft. Then simply roll out your insulation between the joists. Cut where necessary if it's too long or to join sections. The edges do not need to overlap, just butt up against each other.

2 Lay the next layer the other way, ie horizontally across the joists.

3 If you have any electric cables in the loft, carefully lift them to lie on top of the insulation; they should not be left underneath.

* If you have any light fittings in the ceilings below, ensure you leave a gap around them of around 8cm, to ensure they don't overheat. Special hoods can be bought to go over them to prevent fire risk to the insulation and to help prevent a fire below from spreading into the loft.
* Any pipes in the loft must be lagged to prevent them from freezing, as the loft space will now be significantly cooler.
* In addition, your water tank needs special care for the same reason – don't lay insulation under your tank, and install a purpose-built jacket over the tank to protect it from the cold and prevent it from freezing in winter.

Financial help

At the time of writing, discussions are being held with the government on grants and loans being made available to put towards the cost of insulating homes. It is likely this will be in the region of £2,000 per home, with a limit on the number of applications that will be accepted, so get in early. For more information check out the Energy Saving Trust's website (energysavingtrust.org.co.uk). A word of warning is that many builders will try and capitalise on this and tender for the business – so make sure you choose a reputable company such as www.awomanstouch.org.uk to conduct your insulation, and give you peace of mind.

Fire prevention

Having redecorated several homes following fires, and seen the devastation it causes to people's lives and possessions, this is definitely a subject to take extremely seriously and do everything you can to prevent it from happening to your home.

Smoke alarms

This is definitely an area where prevention is by far a preferable option to cure. My other half is a fireman (yes I know, I'm a very lucky girl!) and some of the things that he and his colleagues have to contend with are quite horrific, shocking and scary – and could have been easily avoided.

However, you can all benefit from his knowledge now, as he's helped me to write this next section so that we are all as well-informed as possible on the subject. Here are some sensible precautions:

* Have a fire blanket and fire extinguishers in high-risk areas such as the kitchen.
* Make sure the extinguisher is suitable for the type of fire you would be dealing with – for example a powder extinguisher for electrical fires.
* The most important thing you need is a smoke alarm; without this you may not even wake up if you have a fire. They can be bought from most good DIY stores and cost in the region of £4 each. We all know how sensitive they are – think of how little smoke it takes to set one off when cooking. Smoke alarms are designed to be this sensitive so that they will sound as soon as a fire, or smouldering, starts, giving you as much time as possible to leave the building. Remember you have just a few minutes before a fire can take hold.
* If you live in open-plan accommodation you may experience problems with false alarms, usually caused by cooking fumes. To alleviate this problem consider buying a detector that has a hush facility. With this detector you will be able to silence the alarm for a short period when cooking is taking place.

* Carbon monoxide monitors are also a good idea, and should be located near your boiler to alert you if there is a leak.
* Battery-powered detectors: Never remove the battery from your detector even for a short period; remember, the detector is only doing its job. Most budget smoke detectors will come with a battery ready fitted. This battery will last you for at least one year. Make a point of changing that battery annually. Consider using one of your children's birthdays, or a special occasion, to remind you to change it. More expensive 10-year batteries are now available and if you are intending to stay in your house you should consider purchasing one of these.
* Mains-powered detectors: You may wish to consider a mains-powered detector. Normally, they use power from the mains but in the event of a power cut, a pre-installed battery takes over to ensure you are always protected. These systems use very little electricity and alleviate the problems of flat batteries.
* Fitting smoke alarms: At the present time there is no legislation to force people to have smoke detectors fitted to their homes, although building regulations now insist that smoke detectors be fitted to all new residential accommodation. The minimum recommendation is that you fit at least one smoke alarm to each level of your home. This is the absolute minimum that you should have in your home.
* Positioning of Smoke Alarms: They should ideally be put in every room except for the kitchen and the bathroom – smoke from cooking and steam from hot water can cause false alarms. The minimum should be one smoke alarm on each floor level.
* You should definitely consider installing an alarm in a child's bedroom – which could contain a CD player, computer, television, video, games console, alarm clock and lamp, all of which are potential fire hazards. If the detector is outside the room on the landing and the bedroom door is closed, it will take some time for the smoke from a fire inside the room to get out and reach the detector; the younger children are, the deeper they sleep.
* If you have a spare room where no-one sleeps and there are no electrical appliances in that room, then that room may not need a smoke alarm. Detectors should be sited 30cm from walls and light fittings. This is because light fittings attract dust which can cause false alarms, and sometimes smoke doesn't go right into the corner of the ceiling in the early stages of a fire.

How to react

Remember: Get out! Stay out! Dial 999

When they are at work most people know the actions to take when the fire alarm sounds; they know the route to take out of the building and where to gather together outside so that fire marshals can check registers to see that everyone is accounted for. At no time would you consider deviating from this and going to look for the fire.

At home the story is often very different, with sometimes fatal consequences. When at home we can get used to the alarm going off while someone is cooking, but what do people do when the alarm sounds at two o'clock in the morning?

Often people will go and look to see why the alarm is sounding; they may even open the door to the room with the fire in, and that action will allow the fire to spread quickly around the house, when it could trap them inside or cut them off from the stairs so they can't get back to where their children are sleeping.

Some people manage to leave the house safely and then go back inside, either to save possessions or pets, and they end up being killed or injured. Pets almost always leave the building without the owner realising and virtually all of your possessions will be replaced by your house insurance. The only way to react to a smoke alarm at home at night is to:

* Get up.
* Get everyone in the house together.
* Leave the building by the quickest route, usually down the stairs and out of the front door.
* Dial 999 and ask for the Fire Service.

If you follow the above advice you will survive a fire. It seems so simple, yet still people are killed and injured in fires every day.

Kerrie's top tip

* Once a week test the battery: press the button until the alarm sounds.
* Twice a year open the case and gently vacuum the inside to remove dust from the sensors. If it doesn't open, vacuum through the holes.
* Once a year change the battery (unless it's a 10 year battery).
* After 10 years replace your alarm with a whole new unit.

Installing a smoke alarm

1 Having used a detector to check for wires or pipes, mark the position for your alarm.

2 Drill holes to the correct depth. then insert wall plugs.

3 Put the screws in place but do not screw them in completely.

4 Fix the alarm in position and tighten the screws.

5 Put the battery in place and test to check that it works (and read the tip box opposite).

APPENDIX

Glossary

Allen key – a small metal tool with a hexagonal end, available in different sizes, to fit and turn specific size Allen screws.

Architrave – a moulding, for decorative purposes, which is positioned over the joint of a door frame and the wall.

Bath panel – a panel, usually removable for plumbing maintenance, which fits along the side of the bath to hide the pipe work beneath.

Block – building material used to build walls in place of (smaller) bricks.

Boxing In – a way to cover up unattractive areas such as piping, and built using a frame of battens and board attached. Can then be painted to blend into surrounding area.

Bradawl – a small hand held pointed tool used, for example, to make pilot holes in wood.

Caulk – a filler used in decorating for cracks in corners or around windows/doors. It can be painted over when dry.

Cavity Wall – the wall of a house where there is a gap (cavity) between two layers of brick or block. This can be filled with cavity wall insulation such as polystyrene to insulate a home more effectively.

Ceiling rose – see rose.

Chipboard – a board which is made in sheets from compressed wooden fibres with a rough finish.

Cistern – a tank that stores water, commonly for a toilet, but also refers to a large water tank, normally found in a loft, which supplies water for a whole house.

Concrete – a building material made from cement, sand and aggregate and water that sets to a hard, stone-like finish.

Condensation – a term used to describe the moisture that forms on cold surfaces such a mirrors and windows, when the air in a room becomes saturated, such as after a hot shower in a bathroom.

Consumer unit – the box of electrics which contains the fuses or circuit breakers for your home, and the main isolating switch. Generally located near the front door and close to the meter.

Cornice – decorative moulding attached to the joint between the ceiling and the wall. A more ornate version of coving.

Coving – a concave, plain moulding, attached to the joint between the ceiling and the wall. A cornice is a more ornate type of coving.

Cutting-in – applying paint by brush to a wall or ceiling around joints or obstacles such as windows and doors, before rolling the wider, flat areas.

Dado rail – usually made of wood this is a rail that runs around a room at approximately waist height. It can be used to divide the colour of a wall, often using a darker colour below to hide more wear and tear.

Damp-proof course (DPC) – a layer of plastic which is laid on top of a course of bricks while the wall is being built, just above ground level, to stop water from soaking into the wall.

Dry lining – an alternative to plastering, where plasterboard is attached to a metal or wooden framework on the wall, and the joints of the boards are then taped and filled to leave a smooth surface ready for painting.

Emulsion – water-based paint ideal for covering large areas of a room such as a ceiling or walls.

Flat-pack – the way many items of furniture such as bookshelves or desks are bought from the shop. They need to be assembled at home, and usually all the fittings and screws required are provided within the pack.

Flush – term to denote a smooth, level surface where two surfaces meet (for example a flush light switch lies flat to the surrounding wall).

Fuse – a safety device used in electrics. When the fuse reaches a certain temperature due to the level of current passing through, the wire melts cutting the circuit.

Gloss – an oil-based hard wearing paint generally used on wood and metal, which dries to a high sheen.

Grout – material used to fill the gaps between tiles. It usually comes in powder form and is mixed with water.

Hardboard – a board which is relatively thin, with one smooth side and one rough side. Generally used for preparing floors for their final covering.

Knotting solution – a solution that is painted over knots in wood to prevent their sap from bleeding through subsequent layers of paint.

Lath and Plaster – an old fashioned method for finishing a wall. The laths are interwoven and nailed to the joists and the plaster, often containing horse hair to bind it, is then applied on top, and can be painted when dry.

Laying off – light brush strokes, made in a similar direction, to eliminate brush stokes left on a painted surface.

Lintel – a solid piece of wood, metal or concrete which spans the opening of a door or window to support the wall above.

MDF – a board material, full name Medium Density Fibreboard, useful for making cupboards, shelves and for boxing in.

Mitre block – a tool designed to aid cutting mitre joints for skirting boards or coving, it is generally a pieces of wood, or a device with clamps, into which the item to be cut is inserted and a specific angle is held for cutting to ensure a snug fit for internal and external corners.

Nogging – name given to the small horizontal pieces of wood between upright joists/studs which help stabilise the wall.

Oil-based – term used when referring to the make up of paint.

Picture rail – a decorative moulding, usually made from wood, attached to the wall approximately 4/5th of the way up to the ceiling. Historically this was used to hang pictures from on long wires, but more commonly used today in a similar way to a dado rail, as a way to break up the wall and give the opportunity to use a different wall colour above and below.

Pilot hole – a small hole made or drilled as a guide for either further drilling, or for a nail or screw to be inserted directly.

Plaster – the material used to plaster a wall, which comes in powder form and is mixed with water and applied using a trowel. When dry it can be painted.

Plasterboard – an alternative to plastering, used in dry lining, this is a board that is constructed of two sheets of strong paper with a layer of plaster in-between, and can be neatly cut to fit specific areas and shapes.

Plumb – term denoting an upright, often achieved using a plumb line or spirit level.

Plywood – a board material manufactured by placing thin veneers of wood at right angles to each other. Used in preparation of floors for final covering and general building.

Pointing – the area of mortar visible between bricks in a wall, which is smoothed into an attractive finish by a brick layer using a special tool.

Profile gauge – a special tool for copying the shapes of objects and transferring them to tiles for cutting.

Primer – the first to be applied to a bare surface in its preparation for painting.

Putty – substance made from linseed oil, which is used to hold glass in place in wooden or metal frames. Easily mouldable, it dries solid over time and can be painted.

PVA – polyvinyl acetate used for example, diluted, to seal a freshly plastered wall before painting to prevent paint absorption.

Rose – term for the plastic or plaster area around a ceiling light fitting.

RSJ – rolled steel joist, used as a structural support in building.

Scrim – name for the tape used to join sheets of plaster board when dry lining.

Sealant – a water proof filler, also known as silicone or mastic, used to fill gaps between surfaces such as tiles and a bath.

Skim – term used to describe the application of the final smooth coat of plaster to a wall or ceiling.

Skirting board – the usually wooden moulding that is fixed to the bottom of a wall where it meets the floor, and serves a protective as well as decorative purpose.

Soil pipe – the large pipe that carries waste from the toilet to the sewage system. It is usually fixed to the outside of a house but can sometimes be boxed in internally.

Spacer – small plastic item used in tiling to keep consistent gaps between tiles into which grout is later applied.

Spirit level – generally metal, this long thin tool contains a liquid reservoir with a bubble that is used to achieve either vertical or horizontal alignment.

Steam stripper – a machine which generates steam to a flat plate which is held against a papered wall to make the wall paper easier to strip.

Stud wall – usually non structural, a stud wall is made of studs and noggins and finished usually by dry lining or plastering.

Underlay – the layer placed beneath the final flooring layer. This tends to be a cushioned finish under carpets and a waterproof membrane under laminate or wooden floors.

Vinyl emulsion – water-based paint which is slightly hardier than regular emulsion and therefore good for areas that need to be wiped clean.

Wall plug – the plastic plug that is pushed into a drilled hole in the wall in order to hold a screw in place. Can also be made from metal, particularly those designed for use on stud walls, which have a butterfly mechanism to attach themselves to the back of the plasterboard for a more secure fixing.

Index

A

Allen keys 10
Architraves 72-73
Augers 106-107
A Woman's Touch 7

B

Bathrooms 132-133, 144
   flooring 79
   lighting 121
   tiling 138-141
Blinds 85
Boilers – see Heating
   and Water systems
Buckets 58
Builders 23
Building extensions 23

C

Carbon monoxide
   detectors 31, 152
Carpenters 22
Carpet laying 65
Caulk – see fillers
Ceilings 46-50
   lights 120-121
Cleaning products, cloths
   and sponges 36, 58
Compost 36
Condensation 144, 151
Connaught Hotel 7
Cornices and roses 136
Coving 49, 136-137
Curtain poles and
   tracks 84-85

D

Damp 46, 144-145, 149
   penetrating 145
   rising 145
   traumatic 145
Doors 54-55, 83, 88-91, 94-97
   draughtproofing 150
   flush 54
   handles 90-91
   hinge fixings 91
   internal 88
   lighting 120
   locks 94
   mortice bolts 95-96
   panel 54-55
   sticking 89
   trimming to size 68, 88-89
Draughts 97, 150
Drilling 95-96, 140
Dripping overflow pipe 108
Dry lining 21
Dust sheets and cloths 13, 44

E

Electric appliances 29, 37,
   114, 122
   dishwashers and
     washing machines
     37,103-105
   checking water pipes 33
   codes 105
   connecting 104
   not working 123
Electrical tape 12
Electrical system 19, 22,
   26-29,113-123
   consumer units 27-28,
     114, 118, 120, 122-123
   earth wire 114, 119
   Feed-in Tariff scheme 37
   fuse box 27
   heating 34
   in 'wet' rooms 113
   lighting circuit 28-29
   miniature circuit breakers
     (MCB) 27
   not working 123
   radial circuit (high wattage)
     28-29
   regulations 26, 114
   Residual Current Device
     (RCD) 27
   ring circuit (sockets) 28-29
   safety 26-27, 114
   socket covers 116-117
   wire colours 114
Electricians (certified) 22,
   113, 122
Electricity meter 26
   taking readings 26
Electricity terminology 29
   Amps 29
   Volts 29
   Watts 29, 114
Energy Saving Trust 37, 151
Extension leads 122
Extractor fans 144

F

Fairtrade products 37
Fillers and caulk 44, 46-47
Fires and prevention 19, 88,
   152-153
   fire blankets and
     extinguishers 145, 152
   how to react 153
First aid kit 145
Flex 115, 122
Floors and flooring 65-81
   around pipes and odd
     shapes 79-80

beading 73
concrete 69
   filling gaps between
   floorboards 66
   hardboard base 68-69
   laminate 70-71
   calculating quantity 70
   MDF base 68
   plywood base 68
   preparation 68, 74-75
   sanding 67
   sealing edges 79
   squeaky boards 66
   staining or
     varnishing 67
   tiles 74-77
   underlay 70-71
     fibreboard 70
     membrane 70
   uneven floors 68
   vinyl 78-81
   wooden 66--68
Floor sanders 17, 67
Forest Stewardship
   Council 37
Fuses 29, 114-115, 120,
   122-123
   blown 123
   rewirable 123

G

Gardening 36
Gas appliances 30
Gas fitters 22, 31
   Gas Safe (ex-Corgi
     Scheme) 31
Gas system 30-31
   fumes 31
   heating 35
   meter 30
   mains tap 31
   smell 31
Glaziers 23
Grab adhesives 134
Gutters and waste pipes 33
   leaky 145

H

Handywomen 23
Heat loss 150
Heat pumps 34, 37
Heating system (see
   also Water system
   and Radiators) 34-35
   back boilers 34
   biomass boilers 34
   central heating 34-36
   combi boilers 34

   condensing boilers
     34-35, 37
   storage heaters 34
   traditional boilers 34
   underfloor 34
   wood stoves 37
Heave 146
Hiring tools 17, 45, 67
House saving kit 145

I

Infestation of pests 148-149
   precautions 149
Insulation 36, 144, 150-151
   financial help 151
   loft 150-151
Insurance 22, 92, 146, 153

K

Kitchens 144, 152
   changing cupboard
     doors 128-129
   flooring 79
   lighting 120
   misaligned cupboard
     doors 129
   tiling 138-141
Knocking through
   walls 23
Knotting 44, 47

L

Ladder hooks and
   stand-offs 45
Ladders and stepladders
   13, 45, 48-49
Leaking taps 100-101
   changing washers
     100-102
   disk valves 101
   O rings 102
Lighting 36, 118-123
   bathroom 121
   bedroom 120
   ceiling lights 120
   circuit 28-29
   compact fluorescent
     lamps (CFLs) 119
   energy saving bulbs 19
   fittings 120
   halogen bulbs 119
   LED lights 119
   not working 123
   switches 49, 118-119
   traditional bulbs 119
   trouble shooting 123
   lamps and candles 118
Loft conversions 23

M
Masking tape 12, 39, 44, 52, 55
Mitre blocks 134, 136-137
Mould 144

P
Paint brushes 43, 45, 48
Paint kettles 45, 48
Paint pads 51
Paint rollers and trays 43, 45, 50
    extension poles 50
    radiator 51
Paint types 40-42
    emulsion 40, 42, 48, 50
    oil-based (solvent-based) 41-43, 50, 52
    primers 42, 47
    top coat (gloss) 42, 53
    undercoat 42
    water-based 40-43, 50
Painters and decorators 21
Painting 21, 40-55
    colour divisions 55
    cutting in 48-49
    doors 54-55
    order of painting 54
    how many coats? 50
    masking areas 52
    preparation 44, 46-47
    radiators 53
    rolling 48-51
    windows 52-53
        order of painting 52-53
    woodwork 47, 49, 52-55
Papering brushes 59, 61
Paste table, folding 58
Pencils and note pad 10, 58
Picture hooks and hanging 63, 130-131
Planning permission 23, 37
Plasterers 21
Plastering 21
Plumbers 22
Plumbing 99-111
Plumb line 58
Plungers 106
Power cuts 122-123
Professional help 20-21, 86, 113, 122
Protective equipment 18-19
    face masks 18, 47, 67, 151
    footwear 19
    gloves 18, 151
    goggles 18, 46, 67, 151
    overalls 19, 151
    Radiators (see also Heating and Water systems) 53, 111
    bleeding 35, 111
    corrosion 35
    keys 111
    servicing 35
    thermostatic valves 111

R
Ramsey, Gordon 7
Recycling 36
Resealing bath and basin edges 132-133

S
Safety 13, 18-19
    clothing 18-19, 151
    electrical 27, 114, 122
    gas 30-31
    hazards 19
    ladder 13-14
    long hair 19
Sandpaper and block 44, 47, 67
Scaffold boards 45
Scissors 58, 61-62
Security 88, 92-95, 120
Shelving 126-127
    adjustable 127
    floating 126
Shower heads 111
Silicone sealant 132-133
Sinks and drains 33, 106-107
    chemical cleaners 36, 106-107
    plug strainer 106
    unblocking 106-107
Skirting boards 49, 134-135
Smoke alarms 152-153
    installing 153
    testing 153
Solar energy and heating 34, 37
Spirit level 10, 39, 68, 78, 119, 126-127
Stains 46
Stairwells 13, 120
Steel/straight rules 10, 58, 63, 69
Stencils 40
Subsidence 146
Sugar soap 44, 46

T
Tape measure 10, 58
Taps 100-102
    dripping 100-102
    kitchen (mixer) 102
    traditional 101
Tile cutters 74
    electric 74, 76
    manual 74, 77
Tilers 21
Tiling 21
    cutting 76-77, 139
    floors 74-77
    grouting 77, 139-141
    replacing 140-141
    spacers 139
    walls 138-141
Toilet seat changing 133
Tool box 11

Tools 10-17, 114, 136, 145
    bradawls 11, 14
    brick bolster 140
    caring for 43
    chisels 11, 16, 96, 140
    craft knife 11, 17, 63
    drills and bits 12, 14-15, 95
        ceramic 140
        corded vs cordless 15
    electric drills 14-15
    filling knives 44
    flooring 70, 78
    grout scraper 140
    hacksaws 11
    hammers 10, 16
    jigsaw 70
    nail guns 69
    painting 43-45
    planes 17
    plasterboard saw 12
    pliers 11, 114
    plumbing 100
    putty knife 87
    saws 16
    scrapers 44
    screwdrivers 10, 17, 114
        insulated 116-117, 120
    shave hooks 44
    silicone remover 132
    spanners 11, 17
    Stanley knife 69, 132
    tile saw 74, 76
    tiling 78
    wall papering 58-59
Torches 145
Toxic substances 19, 36

V
Ventilation 140

W
Wall fixings 12
    hollow wall plugs 131
    wall plugs (Rawlplugs) 12, 14-15, 121, 126-127, 130-131, 135
Wallpapering 39, 56-63
    around sockets and switches 63
    around windows 62
    corners of rooms 62
    hanging 60-63
    lining 56
    over hooks and screws 63
    preparation 58-59
    quantity of rolls 57
    stripping previous paper 59
Wallpaper stripper 59
Wallpaper types
    embossed 56-57
    flock 56
    hand-printed 56

    standard pattern 56
    washable 57
    woodchip 56-57
Walls 46-51, 58
    cavity 150
    cracks 47, 146
    masonry 135
    new plaster 60
    sizing bare plaster 58
    stud/hollow 131, 135
Wastewater and sewage 32-33
    low-flush toilets 36
Water butts 36
Water system (see also Heating system and Radiators) 32-35, 100, 103
    ballcocks 108-109
    cisterns 33, 35, 108-109
        replacing a valve 109
    direct plumbing system 32, 35
    frozen pipes 110
    hard water 33
    hot water 34-35
    indirect plumbing system 32, 35
    isolation valve 100, 105
    lagging cylinders and pipes 33, 151
    leaking pipes 110
    main stop cock and valves 32-33, 100
    meters 32
    noisy pipes and boiler 35, 110
    outside taps 33
    pipe detector – see Wire and pipe detector
    tank insulation 151
    turning off 100
Waterproof tape 145
Websites 20, 22, 31, 37, 122, 151
Wedges 70-71, 90
White spirit 47
Windows 52-53, 83-87, 92-93, 97
    casement 92-93, 97
    double glazing 150
    draughtproofing 150
    locks and keys 92-93
    rattling 97
    replacing glass 86-87, 150
    sash 53, 93, 97
    stay locks 92-93
    sticking 97
Wire and pipe detector 13-14, 29, 126-127, 131, 134, 137
Wiring a plug 115
Wood decay 147
    dry rot 147
    wet rot 147

Author's acknowledgements

I would like to thank my amazing husband Stuart Eade, for his unyielding support whilst I wrote this book, both morally and later physically by taking our new baby out of the house so I could concentrate! Also my dad, John Hanafin, for setting me on the road to DIY in the first place some 25 years ago, and for selflessly sharing his knowledge with me, and his dad's home-made tools. I would like to thank my mum Wendy Hanafin, who's trust in my decision to leave a well paid job and go it alone in the building trade helped to give me the confidence to succeed, and also Tina Turnbull, who has pretty much run A Woman's Touch single handed whilst I've been tied up with the book and the baby! Finally, thank you to the following people who helped to check all my words – Jane Ringe, Rose Lock, Barry Eade, Leona Hodson, Dimple Sthankiya and Rod Younger.

Author:	Kerrie Hanafin
Managing editor:	Louise McIntyre
Designer:	Richard Parsons
Photographer:	Terry Donovan
Copy editor:	Chris Maillard
Index:	Peter Nicholson

Haynes Publishing would like to thank the following for their help in producing this manual

Naomi Buckland
Paul Buckland
Terry Donovan
Draper Tools
Emma Jones
Georgie Loder
Pete Shoemark
Christine Smith
Elaine Sparkes
Gill and Mat Sparkes
Spiller Architectural Ironmongery
Nigel Tate
Mark Tampling